VIDEO GAMES

VIDEO GAMES

A Popular Culture
Phenomenon

Arthur Asa Berger

TRANSACTION PUBLISHERS
New Brunswick (U.S.A.) and London (U.K.)

Third printing 2009

Copyright © 2002 by Transaction Publishers, New Brunswick, New Jersey.

Library of Congress Catalog Number: 2001058538
ISBN: 978-0-7658-0913-1
Printed in the United States of America

Library of Congress Cataloging-in-Publication Data

Berger, Arthur Asa, 1933-
   Video games: a popular cultural phenomenon / Arthur Asa Berger.
       p. cm.
   Includes bibliographical references (p.) and index.
   ISBN 0-7658-0102-7 (cloth: alk. paper)—ISBN 0-7658-0913-3 (paper: alk. paper)
     1. Video games—Social aspects. 2. Video games—psychological aspects.
   I. Title.

GVI469.34.S63   B47   2002
306.4'87—dc21   2001058538

Contents

Preface   vii

Acknowledgments   ix

Part 1: Theoretical Concerns

1. Video Games: A Popular Culture Phenomenon   3
2. Narratives in the Electronic Age   29
3. Video Games as Cultural Indicators   49
4. A Bio-Psycho-Social Perspective on Video Games   55

Part 2: Analyzing Representative Games

5. *Myst, Riven,* and the Adventure Video Game   73
6. *Lara Croft* and the Problem of Gender in Video Games   83
7. *Half-Life* and the Problem of Monsters   93
8. Conclusions   105

Bibliography   113

Index   115

Preface

It was in 1984 that I first became interested in the video game phenomenon. I had read a number of articles about *Pac-Man* in various newspapers and magazines and I sensed that something rather interesting was going on with video games . . . but I didn't know what it was. I had played *Pong* and *Pac-Man,* and in 1984 I wrote my first article on video games—a "think piece" essay for the *Los Angeles Times* on the *Pac-Man* phenomenon. Over the years I followed the development of these games in the popular press and then, in 1998 I started investigating them seriously. I checked them out on the Internet and got a subscription to a video game magazine and I corresponded with people at some video game websites.

In 1999 I was invited to attend a conference on children's literature in Germany and was given an assignment—to see how children's narratives were being affected as they moved from print to electronic media. I wrote a paper for the conference, which, in slightly modified form, is the second chapter in this book. My research for this paper led me to write this book. I purchased a number of books on video games, bought some video games, started playing them (with questionable success) and started doing research on the whole phenomenon. I was fortunate enough to be able to interview some video game makers at Lucas Arts, and I also corresponded with some scholars who had done work on video games and journalists who worked at video game sites.

The result of my effort is the book you are about to read.[1] My focus is not on the quality of the game play or matters like that, but, broadly speaking, on the social, psychological, and cultural significance of this new entertainment phenomenon. I hope you will find this book instructive and, given the nature of my subject, also illuminating and entertaining.

Note

1. It takes between nine months and a year to publish a book in print once it has been accepted by a publisher. Because the video game industry changes so quickly, it is impossible for me, therefore, to be up-to-date on some of the matters I discuss. When I wrote my book, in 2000, Sega looked like it would survive and the producers of the *Tomb Raider* film were trying to figure out who to cast as Lara Croft. By the time I got the copy-edited version of my manuscript, in June 2001, Sega had stopped making video game consoles and Tomb Raider, starring Angelina Jolie, was about to be released. These matters, which involve video game console wars and other such things, keep changing. But my socio-cultural analysis of the video game phenomenon and of the video games I deal with are not affected by changes in the industry. Probably the best way to keep your finger on the pulse of the video game industry is to follow it on the Internet. *Video Games: A Popular Culture Phenomenon* offers insights into the significance of the video game phenomenon and some of its most celebrated games.

Acknowledgments

I would like to thank the many scholars and journalists who were kind enough to help me with this book and to the people I met at Lucas arts, who gave me important insights into the video game industry. In particular, I'd like to thank Janet H. Murray, Henry Jenkins, Brenda Laurel, George Landow, Lauren Fielding, Michael Brown, and Freedom Baird for their suggestions and to thank Kitty O'Neil and Mike McCormick from Lucas Learning and Haden Blackman from Lucas Arts.

Part 1

Theoretical Concerns

1

Video Games:
A Popular Culture Phenomenon

> *"Each successive generation of video games has become more technologically sophisticated, more realistic, and more violent. The newest wave of video games, based on CD-ROM technology (the same technology people use for music recordings and computer software), is, in fact becoming more like film and television than what we traditionally expect of a video game. This is a major evolutionary step beyond the simple graphics of the classic* Space Invaders *arcade game so popular fifteen or twenty years ago, or the tiny animated cartoon figures of the Nintendo system that have dominated the video game market in recent years."*
> —Eugene F. Provenzo, Jr. (Steinberg and Kincheloe, eds. 1997: 104)

In this book I deal with video games, a popular entertainment phenomenon (with a focus on adventure or action-adventure video games) in terms of their social, psychological, and cultural significance. I also consider the size of the video game industry, new developments in video game player technology, and how video games have affected story telling—and in this regard, compare narratives in print and video games. To accomplish these goals, I do the following things:

1. I consider what video games are and how they relate to play;
2. I discuss whether video games are an art form or a new medium,

3. I say something about the nature of narrativity;
4. I examine the role video games play in the lives of young children, and discuss how to analyze their cultural significance;
5. I offer a bio-psycho-social analysis of the video game phenomenon;
6. I analyze four of what are generally considered to be the most important adventure video games of recent years: *Myst, Riven, Tomb Raider,* and *Half-Life.*
7. I support my analyses by using quotations from many experts and authorities in the field.

A News Event of Significance for Gamers

On October 26, 2000, Sony introduced its PlayStation 2 video game machine in the United States—a device that it believes will revolutionize home entertainment. Sony considers the PlayStation 2 (also known as the PS2) a "Trojan horse," that will be purchased as a video game player but will eventually change the way Americans entertain themselves in general. That is because the PlayStation 2, which sells for $299, also can play DVD films, music CD-ROMs, and video games that were purchased to be played on the PlayStation 1. (Sony is losing around one hundred dollars on each console sold in the United States, but will make up its losses on the consoles from its profits on the video games and in licensing fees.) The PlayStation 2 also has a port for a hard drive and another port that will enable it to support a high-speed Internet connection. It will also, when add-ons are developed, let its owners make music mixes and edit their own digital movies.

There are some questions about whether the Sony PlayStation 2 can actually become the center of household entertainment in America. But even if it doesn't, it will unquestionably be a major force in the video game industry. We must remember that Sony is building on an enormous base: there are estimates that the Sony PlayStation 1 is found in one out of every six households in the United States. (Sony has sold something like 27 million PlayStation 1 consoles here in the United States and 75 million worldwide.) I will discuss the different consoles used to play video games, which compete with the PS2, in more detail later in the book.

Most Americans are well aware of the existence of video games. There are occasionally articles about new video games in newspapers and the *New York Times* regularly carries a feature on new video

games every Thursday in its "Circuits" section. There are also arti
on the industry and various games in magazines such as *Time*
Newsweek, and there are many magazines devoted to video games,
and hundreds (if not thousands) of Internet sites on every conceivable
aspect of video games.

Many video game companies have their own sites where you can
find a great deal of information about specific games. If you take
interactivity as one of the main constituents of video games, there are
also a number of interactive image-less fiction narratives, what might
be thought of as an elite art form version of the video game without
animated characters. So, there is a continuum of games that covers
everything from relatively crude "bang-em-up" wrestling games to
ingenious science fiction and adventure games to postmodern avant-
garde novels.

Are Video Games an Art Form or a New Medium?

There is some confusion about what video games are. Are they an
art form with many different genres, similar in nature to the novel, or
some kind of new medium? There are decent arguments that can be
made for both positions. Video games are interactive, but there are
other texts and media that are interactive, so I don't think interactivity
means that video games should be considered a new medium—unless
interactivity is enough to qualify anything as a new medium. The
novel is an art form using the medium of print (but now also, with the
development of e-books, electronic media) that has many different
genres—everything from genre stories such as mysteries and science
fiction stories to non-formulaic, non-genre stories about individuals
and their relationships. Thus, there is a wide spectrum of novels—
everything from tough guy mysteries like Mickey Spillane's *I, the
Jury* to James Joyce's *Ulysses.* I would like to suggest that video
games are probably best understood to be similar to the novel in that
there are many different genres of video games; both novels and video
games are, then, from my perspective, art forms.

When scholars write about video games, they often use the term
"form" to discuss them. For example, Jay David Bolter and Richard
Grusin write, in their book *Remediation: Understanding New Media,*

> The term *computer game* covers a range of forms, including violent action games,
> role-playing and narrative games, erotic and frankly pornographic applications,

card games, puzzles and skill-testing exercises, and educational software. Some of these forms are clear repurposings of early games. . . . Computer games are delivered on a variety of platforms . . . in all their forms and with all their modes of delivery, digital games illustrate the commodification of the computer. (2000, 89)

The authors use the term remediation to deal with the ways in which new media refashion prior media forms. This concept may help us understand how to categorize video games.

Another author, Eugene F. Provenzo, also uses the term "form" in dealing with video games. He writes in his essay "Video Games and the Emergence of Interactive Media for Children" (in Steinberg and Kinchloe, 1997, 103):

I argue here that video games represent a new frontier for media in our culture. Video games are a complex and rapidly evolving form—one that most parents and adults pay relatively little attention to.

Authors use the term "form" because there are so many different genres of video games. Just having different genres, however, is not a proof that we are dealing with an art form. Media such as film, radio, and television also have many different genres, so there is a logic to arguing that video games are a new medium. I would suggest that because video games are played on television screens or computer monitor screens, and thus use an "old" medium, it makes sense to think of video games as art forms. The issue is not, from my point of view, a terribly important one. What is most important is that we analyze video games and try to understand their impact on the people who play them and on society at large.

We can think of each video game as a text, a work of popular art that is created collectively (like films and television programs). Video games are created by teams of writers, artists, musicians, and various kinds of other technicians. In critical parlance works of art are called "texts," to make it easier for writers and scholars to talk about them without having to name them or describe them every time. These video games are created by authors (teams of writers and artists) and are created in a particular society, directed toward a specific audience, and played on a familiar medium—the television screen or computer monitor screen.

We can see these relationships better by putting them into a chart of what I call the focal points involved in analyzing mass mediated texts.

Let me deal with these focal points in a bit more detail. A video

Video Games: A Popular Culture Phenomenon

FIGURE 1.1
Focal Points in the Study of Texts

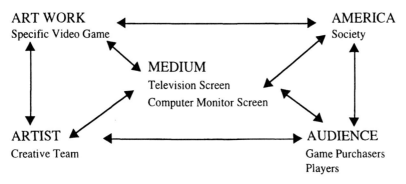

game is distributed on different kinds of devices that contain software such as CD-ROMs, cartridges, or DVD disks. The software is, in my scheme of things, the work of art, or in this case, the specific game. For example, there are five CD-ROMs needed to play *Riven*. A particular game is created for a specific audience—gamers who like certain kinds of game. Thus, some gamers love sports video games, others like simulations, others like action-adventure video games, and so on. Of course those who create and manufacture a video game always hope that players who like other kinds of games might be induced to purchase the game they have created and play it, also.

The video game is created and manufactured in some society and often reflects, in subtle and sometimes not easily recognized ways, the beliefs and value systems of the society in which it is made. These values are filtered through the personalities, social class, beliefs, and values of those who actually design and create the game. This means that works of art, in all media, always contain elements of the personalities and life experiences of their makers and also of the societies in which their makers grew up. Video games are played in many countries, so they have to also relate to the interests of players all over the world. For example, many popular video games are created in Japan but are popular in the United States and in many other countries. Video game makers must keep in mind the nature of their audiences—in particular how old the players will be—and their particular interests.

Finally, the art work/text/video game is transmitted by some medium. In the case of video games, as their name suggests, video games are played on video display monitors—either on television sets that are hooked up to game playing consoles or on computer video display monitors in the case of PC video games.

I mentioned, earlier, that there are particular audiences for video games. That explains why there are many different genres or kinds of video games. If you take an art form such as the popular novel, you see that there are many different genres of popular fiction, such as detective novels, science fiction novels, romance novels, spy novels, western novels, and adventure novels.

The same applies to video games; there are many different genres of video games such as action adventure, sports, science fiction, simulations, and role-playing.

It is difficult, at times, to assign a particular genre to a video game because in recent years video game designers have mixed genres together, in the same way that many novelists have. As Michael Brown, an editor at CNET'S Gamecenter (HYPERLINK http://*www.gamecenter*) explained to me in an e-mail message:

> Categorizing computer and video games is becoming increasingly difficult, because in an effort to build unique games, developers are blurring genres together. It used to be that in an "action" game, you'd run around and blow things up. In a role-playing game, you'd go on quests and develop your characters' skills along the way. But now there are action-RPGs, like *System Shock 2*, and adventure-action games, like *Mask of Eternity*. It's a good thing for gaming, but it does make our jobs more difficult when we try to categorize games. (Feb. 8, 2000)

Trying to decide which genre a given game should be put in is worth doing, since it tells us something about the nature of the game, but we must keep in mind that as in other kinds of texts, sometime a game has elements of several different genres in it. For example, many games are combinations of action and adventure or adventure and role playing, though usually one of the two blended genres is dominant.

I think it makes good sense to think of video games as a kind of text that comes in many different genres and blended genres—and thus as an art form—rather than seeing video games as a new medium. There are many video artists who use video to make texts of all kinds, some of which are very avant garde. These texts are not games, however.

New Technologies Make a Difference in Video Games

So the medium of video is not the only important thing as far as understanding what video games are. The important thing, from my point of view as a popular culture critic, is to analyze the video game phenomenon and certain important video games and see what they tell us about ourselves. What has happened is that as the technology of video games has evolved, from diskettes to CD-ROMs and DVD disks, the nature or power of the games has changed considerably. The technical quality of the images and sounds in these games has improved to such a point that it can be suggested that they represent something relatively new in the entertainment world—*interactive narrative texts with multi-dimensional characters.* These texts now have the capacity to involve players to an extent unknown in earlier days, when the technology of these games was much more primitive.

It is important to have an understanding of what interactivity is—a subject I will be discussing at various places in this book. J. C. Herz offers an interesting explanation of interactivity in her book *Joystick Nation: How Videogames Ate Our Quarters, Won Our Hearts, and Rewired Our Minds.* She tells us that video game designers often create their worlds first and then worry about characters and plots and adds that it isn't digital cinematography that makes stories immersive, but something else:

> What makes it [a video game] immersive is a world where no territory is off-limits, anything you see is fair game, and all your actions have consequences. This is what game designers calls a "realtime object-oriented environment," which is to say time moves ahead and the world churns even in places you don't care to look (or haven't found). Characters exist independently. Options shift. Events—some completely beyond your control—unfold in a world that can age . . . .with each tick of its internal clock, the fictional world changes. (1997, 155)

The remarkable developments in video game technology have led to what, one might suggest, is a new (or, perhaps radically transformed is more accurate) entertainment form. It is one that now closely approximates film in terms of the qualities of images and sounds generated by the new video games devices but it is different from film in that players now can immerse themselves into the film-quality texts and participate in them.

This represents, one might argue, a considerable change in our narrative conventions. Reader response theorists have argues that readers y a role in the "creation" of literary texts, in the sense that they help ᴜᴏɪɴg them into being when they read them. With video games, the very notion of authorship becomes problematical, now that gamers have the capacity to affect what happens in a game. That is the point that Ted Friedman makes in his article "Making Sense of Software: Computer Games and Interactive Textuality" (Jones, 1995). He argues that the "oppositions" reading and writing now are connected and it is impossible to determine where one ends and the other begins. Friedman quotes a computer game critic, Orson Scott Card (*Compute,* "Gameplay: Films can make lousy games." 1991:54):

> What every good game author eventually has to learn . . . is that computers are a completely different medium, and great computer artworks will only come about when we stop judging computer games by standards developed for other media . . . .You want to do the rebuilding of Atlanta after the war? SimCity does it better than either the book or the movie of *Gone With the Wind.* The computer "don't know nothin' 'bout birthin' babies," but what it does well, it does better than any other medium that ever existed.

Card's point is well worth considering. He uses the term "computer" but we can extend it to mean console video games and Internet ones as well. What's interesting to note is that now films are being made from popular computer games. Films may make "lousy" computer games, as Card asserts, but we don't know yet whether computer games will make "lousy" films! A number of films, of uneven quality, based on video games, have already been made and others, such as one based on *Tomb Raider,* are currently in production.

According to many critics, all texts are related, in various ways, to previous texts (the technical term for this phenomenon is "intertextuality") and to older media; I don't want to suggest that the new video games are totally different from any of the games that were created before them. But the new machines make possible a considerably different game playing experience from earlier games, such as *Pong* and *Pac-Man.* That is the point to be made.

It is fair to argue, I would suggest, that video games, in general, are a new popular culture phenomenon, and the more recent video games are major transformations of the earlier games. We've had video games for something like thirty years, but it is only in recent years, with the development of new consoles with incredible powers, that video games have been able to evolve into much more powerful and sophisticated works. In addition, it is now possible to play video games on the

Internet, so the nature of game playing has changed considerably with this recent development.

In their article "Nintendo and New World Narratives" (Jones, 1995: 61) Mary Fuller and Henry Jenkins write, "Most of the criteria by which we might judge a classically constructed narrative fall by the wayside when we look at these games as storytelling systems." These games, then, are considerably different from earlier ones, due to new developments in game-playing technology and new levels of interactivity that these new technologies make possible, which leads to a new kind of narrative—one that has interactivity and that generates powerful immersive qualities. One thing remains constant, however—you've got to have a good story, with sympathetic characters, conflict and a satisfying resolution. You can have all the new technology in the world, but it won't mean much if you don't have a compelling story.

Defining Play

Let me offer a minor complication here—we *play* games. But what is play? A classic definition of "play" was made by a Dutch historian J. Huizinga, who wrote in his book *Homo Ludens* that play is

> A voluntary activity or occupation executed with certain fixed limits of time and place, according to rules freely accepted but absolutely binding having its aim in itself and accompanied by feelings of tension, joy, and the consciousness that it is different from ordinary life. (1955: 20)

This definition may be somewhat limiting, but it does call our attention to certain aspects of play that are related to games. It seems likely that Huizinga had games in mind when he defined play the way he did; other theorists, I should point out, offer broader definitions of play. Whatever the case, we tend to separate, in our minds, the world of play from the real world.

Brian Sutton-Smith, a scholar who has done a great deal of work on play, adds an interesting insight about the relation of play to the mass media. He writes in his introduction to William Stephenson's *The Play Theory of Mass Communication,*

> we seem to enjoy escape into fantasy and reverie almost as much as we enjoy "reality," and the modern agencies of mass communication are calculated to stimulate those worlds with such extraordinary vividness that we are hardly aware that there has been any change in our status. The signals are so taken for granted, the communication so implicit, we are taken by stealth as in dreams. (1988: xviii)

Sutton-Smith's words are particularly applicable to the world of video games, and point to an interesting phenomenon. When we play video games, there are times when we lose sight of the fact that we are playing a game and the game becomes something incredibly real to us. In reading magazines devoted to video games, we frequently come across a literary concept—"the suspension of disbelief"—that offers a different way of thinking about the same thing Sutton-Smith is writing about. His notion that play and dreams might be related opens up video games, I would suggest, to the same kinds of analysis Freud made of dreams. There are often, let me suggest, deeper meanings to these games than we might imagine. I will explore some of these deeper meanings later in the book when I analyze some important video games.

Defining Video Games

Video games can be understood to be games generally played using either computers or special game players, such as the PlayStation 2 (they really are dedicated computers) that work with television sets. One of the most significant attributes of video games is that they are *interactive*—that is, as I explained earlier, actions by players affect what happens in the game. But what is a game? Actually, it is rather difficult to define games, because there are so many different kinds of games and different matters related to games.

Let me offer a working definition of a game. For our purposes, games—of all kinds, including video games—can be said to have the following general characteristics:

1. *They are entertainments.* People play games to amuse themselves and, in many cases, others. The concept "play" is quite important here—we are momentarily divorced from real life and the consequences of our failures are, therefore, relatively trivial.
2. *There are rules by which players are bound.* These rules cover (or should cover) every aspect of the game and every possibility that might arise when the game is being played.
3. *They often take place in certain locations.* We play games on boards such as those found in *Monopoly* or in specific locations such as those found in video games such as *Riven, Tomb Raider,* and *Sim City.* Some video games take place in a number of different locations. Sports, such as baseball, football, and basket-

ball, are games that take place on fields and courts with pre-scribed dimensions (between the bases in baseball, between the baskets in basketball and between the goal posts in football). Some video games simulate sports such as football and basketball.

4. *There is often a competitive aspect to games.* A player competes with others or competes against himself in various ways. In many games, one wins points for doing certain things or loses points for neglecting or not being able to do certain things. The fact that there is competition in games and that one never can tell how a particular game will turn out, gives them a dramatic aspect that players find intriguing and stimulating. Many video games are now played by groups of competing players.

5. *Games are seen as artificial, as unreal.* On the other hand, they may reflect things about or mirror, in certain ways, real life. For example, a new game, *The Sims,* is a video game that reflects domestic life and its various problems. As Neva Chonin wrote in *The San Francisco Chronicle* (Feb. 5, 2000, page B1), "In the Sims, the player plays God over a neighborhood of jabbering little people, guiding them through their careers, setting up their families and circles of friends, instigating romances and gener-ally making them as crazed or wholesome as he or she wishes." In his book, *The Uses of Enchantment,* Bruno Bettelheim makes a distinction between the unreal and the untrue. Fairy tales, he tells us, are unreal but they are not untrue, and the same could be said of works of narrative fiction in general.

6. *There are many genres or kinds of games.* Some of the more important genres of video games are sports, action-adventure, role-playing, simulations, and teaching.

7. *There is always the possibility of cheating in games.* So one must be on one's guard when playing games with others. Your oppo-nent might cheat or you might cheat "against" yourself, so to speak.

8. *One can stop playing a game when one feels like it.* Thus games are different from "real life" in that they allow for closure—they have beginnings and ends. We can't stop "playing" life when we get bored with it (without dire consequences, that is). This matter of having a beginning and ending is also found in fictional narra-tives in all media. There are, we will see, other similarities be-tween games and stories.

When it comes to certain genres of video games, the "contest" in-volves a story that asks us to achieve some goal, triumphing over adversaries of one kind or another, so action-adventure or narrative video games are not so different from games as we conventionally think of them. These narrative or adventure video games, as I mentioned earlier, are the kinds of games I will be focusing on in this book, though I will discuss other video games as well. In the jargon game players use, these games are adventure games—though sometimes they are also called action-adventure games or adventure-role playing games, because they blend various game genres.

Chris Crawford on the Design of Video Games

Chris Crawford offers a useful definition of video games in his book *The Art of Computer Game Design*. He argues that games have four basic factors—representation, interaction, conflict, and safety. Discussing the first of these, representation, he writes,

> First, a game is a closed formal system that subjectively represents a subset of reality. . . . By "closed" I mean that the game is complete; no reference need be made to agents outside of the game. Some badly designed games fail to meet this requirement. Such games produce disputes over rules, for they allow situations to develop that the rules do not address. . . . A properly designed game precludes this possibility; it is closed because the rules cover all contingencies encountered in the game. (1982: 7)

He uses the term "formal" to suggest that games have explicit rules and the term system to define games as being collections of parts that interact with each other, frequently in complicated ways.

He concludes his definition of games by writing,

> A game creates a subjective and deliberately simplified representation of an emotional reality. A game is not an objectively accurate representation of reality; objective accuracy is only necessary to the extent required to support the player's fantasy. The player's fantasy is the key agent in making the game psychologically real. (1982: 9)

Crawford's point is worth considering. Games aren't models of reality and don't claim to be; what they do is represent an emotional reality that generates the desired fantasies in the minds of players. Thus, criticizing games for not being real or realistic misses the point. Games take certain elements of reality, what Crawford calls a "subset," and provide focus for players and find ways of supporting the

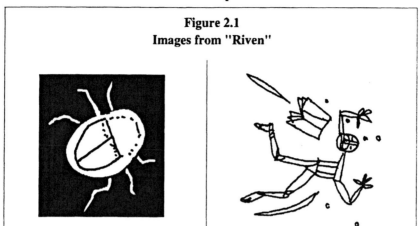

Figure 2.1
Images from "Riven"

fantasies players have. Thus, games are psychologically real in the same way that fictional stories may be made up but can reveal profound truths about human beings and the human condition.

The interactivity in video games is a crucial element in their appeal. What a video game does, Crawford says, is "allow the audience to explore its nooks and crannies to let them generate causes and observe effects." This suggests that video games make players work in two ways: first, players are involved in the events of the game and second, players are also involved in finding out the way the game works.

Crawford offers some important insight into the nature of games in his discussion of the difference between games and stories:

> A story is a collection of facts in a time-sequenced order that suggest a cause and effect relationship. Frequently, the facts presented are deliberately fictitious, because the facts of a story are intrinsically unimportant. Indeed, the entire concept of fiction ("an untruth that is not a lie") only makes sense when one realizes that the facts presented in the fiction are themselves unimportant. The cause and effect relationship suggested by the sequence of facts are the important part of the story. . . . Thus, a story is a vehicle for representing reality, not through its facts per se, but through the cause and effect relationships suggested by the sequence of facts.
>
> Games also attempt to represent reality. The difference between the two is that a story presents the facts in an immutable sequence, while a game presents a branching tree of sequences and allows the player to create his own story by making choices at each branch point. The audience of a story must infer causal relationships from a single sequence of facts; the player of a game is encouraged to explore alternatives, contrapositives, and inversions. The game player is free to explore the causal relationships from many different angles. (1982: 10, 11)

Crawford adds that one of the big problems with adventure video games is that they tend to drag players down a primrose path. By this he means players are ultimately forced to follow the hidden imperatives of the design of the game, but he thinks there are possibilities that designers will figure out ways to design games that actually change as the result of a player's actions, and have surprising resolutions.

This matter of video game players being led down a path is an important one, for it may be that the interactivity in video games is essentially involved with superficial matters and that ultimately all players have to submit to the hidden design elements in the game. Crawford laments that adventure video games don't end with surprises the way print stories do, and those video games (as of the 1980s) that do contain surprises in their resolutions have to limit the freedom of action of players.

All games, Crawford argues, must have conflict in them. If you design a game that doesn't have conflict, you eliminate what he calls "active response" to a player's actions; doing this means, in essence, that you've destroyed the game. Players pursue goals and face obstacles—characters in games who have opposing goals. If you take conflict out of a game, you destroy the reason for interaction and its narrative line; players must deal with some kind of intelligent agents who oppose them and this opposition leads to the interaction. Without this interaction you don't have a game.

One other matter bears consideration. The video games I'm focusing on in this book are called adventure games or sometimes action-adventure or adventure role playing video games and what is important about them is that each of them tells a story. The differences and similarities between print stories and electronic interactive ones (video game stories) is something I will discuss in more detail in the next chapter. To understand video games better, it is useful to consider how they are created. It is to this topic that I now turn.

Espen Aarseth on Creating Video Games

To better understand the nature of these video games, it is useful to know something about how they are created. A Norwegian scholar, Espen J. Aarseth, offers a good description of how video games are created. He writes, in *Cybertext: Perspectives on Ergodic Literature,*

> The formula was simple: take a popular fiction genre, for example the detective novel, create a background story (the more stereotypical the better, since the play-

ers would need less initiation), create a map for the players to move around in, objects to manipulate, characters to interact with, a plot tree or graph with several outcomes, depending on the player's previous decisions, and add descriptions, dialogue, error messages, and a vocabulary for the player. This literary database is accessed via a subprogram called a *parser* that interprets the player's input commands (e.g. hit dragon, eat sandwich, go north). Once an action has been identified, the program changes the database and displays a message about the outcome, until the player quits the game, wins, or "dies" and must start again.

Once the parser and database tools have been developed, these can be reused for several games, and game development then becomes much like planning and writing a piece of short fiction, except that multiple outcomes must be conceived and the players actions (however unreasonable) must be predicted. (1999: 100)

We can see, then, that according to Aarseth there are certain elements that games have: players compete with one another or with others, or with themselves (in terms of beating some kind of time limit). In many games, players control a hero/heroine figure that is commonly known as an *avatar*. If that avatar figure is killed, by opposing characters of one sort or another (aliens, monsters, and so on) the player has to start the game again—and try to avoid getting killed again. The games also generally can be described as belonging to one of a number of different well known genres, such as detective, science fiction, action adventure, horror, sports, or simulations.

There also is the matter of "interactivity"—the way players in a game use animated characters to do things, to act and react to various things that happen in a game. Thus, players identify with certain characters that find themselves facing opponents who want to kill them, want to prevent them from achieving some goal, or want to mislead them—that kind of thing. There is always a choice of actions to take and each choice involves other alternatives as players react to actions and reactions made by their opponents. In an interactive game, what a player does affects the things that happen afterwards in the game. So, at every moment, there are choices to be made and every choice leads to actions by opponents (in narrative games) and then other choices.

There is some question about the degree to which a player really has important choices in games. Video games are designed so that there are elements of choice in them but that is not the same thing as free choice or absolute choice, in which characters can do anything they want to do. There is a set of choices that are open to players at every moment, but these choices, and all choices in video games, are predetermined by the game designers. It is the parser and the design of the video game that determines what we are capable of doing when we play these games! This is an important matter to keep in mind because it qualifies the notion that video games are interactive or limits our notion of what interactivity is all about.

Janet Murray on Holodecks and Interactive Narrative Design

According to Janet Murray, author of a book on interactive fiction and cyberspace, *Hamlet on the Holodeck: The Future of Narrative in Cyberspace,* there are two main structures used in electronic narratives: the *solvable maze* (which often takes the form of a story involving a journey) and the postmodern *tangled rhizome* (in which any point can be connected to any other point, leading to an indeterminate text). She also points out that most interactive narratives follow a basic branching structure that limits the players choice to a selection of alternatives from some kind of a fixed menu. This suggests that interactivity is a much more limited phenomenon than we think it is. One way or another, we have to choose from the options that are open to us and these options are part of the design of the game.

She also considers a question that has been considered earlier in this book—what is the relationship that exists between narratives (stories) and games? Her answer is that stories and games have many things in common and that one of the more interesting narrative structures in interactive fictions is the "contest story," in essence a story with many game elements in it. (Murray, who taught for many years at MIT, has a resource page on the Internet HYPERLINK http://mit/edu/jhmurray/www.HOH.html *http://mit/edu/jhmurray/www.HOH.html* that has many links to articles and other web pages.)

A holodeck, for those who are not familiar with the term, was a device first seen in 1987 in *Star Trek: The Next Generation.* Computers can create elaborate simulations by combining two things—holography and energy-to-matter conversions, which means you have a machine that can create make-believe worlds that can be started and stopped at will. These holodecks are important because they can be seen models, so to speak, for contemporary video games and other kinds of electronic narratives.

The Battle Among the Video Game Console Makers

Video games are generally played on four different platforms:

1. *In arcades,* where the player pays to play a game. The amount of time a typical game lasts in an arcade is a couple of minutes.
2. On *computer monitors,* where the software for the games are on CD-ROMs, DVD disks or on the Internet in the files of a powerful computer (previously, some much simpler games were on 3.25 inch disks, which hold around 1/500th as much data as CD-ROMs).
3. On *television screens,* where the games are played using specially designed game players that use game holding cartridges (such as those from Sega, Sony and Nintendo) and now CD-ROMS and DVD disks. There are also devices now that let players connect to the Internet and play games on their television screens.
4. On *small, portable devices,* such as the Gameboy.

The games on the specially designed players make use of extremely powerful playing devices—typically called video game consoles—such as the Sega Dreamcast and the Sony PlayStation 2, which generate incredible audio-visual effects. These consoles can be thought of, as I suggested earlier, as very powerful dedicated computers—machines designed primarily for playing video games. Engineers have also developed special video and audio cards for computers that greatly enhance their ability to satisfy hard-core and demanding gamers, but these cards are often as expensive or more expensive than a Sega or Sony console.

The companies that produce these video game consoles and players compete with one another ferociously to produce the most powerful device. Until March 4, 2000, the most powerful game player was the Sega Dreamcast, which costs $199. It comes with a modem and software that enables it to connect to the Internet, so a number of video games made for Sega can now be played on the Internet. Sega now gives its Dreamcast away free to players who purchase its Internet service, where they can play games with other gamers or use it to cruise the Internet.

A description of the Sega Dreamcast in *UGODIRECT.COM,* a video game catalogue, reads as follows:

Sega's new awesome Dreamcast is the first 128-bit video gamesystem ever! The system includes a 200-MHz 128-bit processor and is the first console to offer a built-in modem for online gaming, Web browsing, e-mail and chat capabilities. The Dreamcast can display revolutionary new types of realistic and engrossing 3D graphics—human movements, fog, water effects, light and shading appear ultra-realistic. (1999: 4)

The Dreamcast's power is only equaled by computers that cost many times as much as the Dreamcast. It has a very powerful 128-bit microprocessor, powerful audio chips, 3-D graphics capabilities and can also play audio CD-ROMs. Dreamcasts also have Microsoft Windows CE technology in them. (The personal computers that most people use have 32-bit micoprocessors, so these Video Game Consoles, that have 128-bit microprocessors, are extremely powerful devices. The more bits a computer or console has, the more realistic the images it generates can be.)

In Japan, on March 4, 2000 Sony brought out a competing product, the Sony PlayStation II, which cost $360 in Japan; Nintendo is working on a console now called the Game-Cube, which will be available in October 2001. The Sony PlayStation II and the Nintendo Game-Cube will be even more powerful than the Sega Dreamcast Video Console and will also use DVD drives instead of cartridges for the game software, so the consoles can be used to see movies as well as play video games.

In the United States, the Sony PlayStation II, which was just made available on October 26, 2000, sells for $299; the price of the Nintendo Game-Cube is not known yet, but it is unlikely that it will cost more than the PS2. (Sony made an alliance with 7-Eleven stores in Japan to sell its products, so they are widely available there and Sony has sold something like three million PlayStation II consoles in Japan.)

Sony had projected sales of more than two million PlayStation II consoles in the United States the first few weeks following their release. Because of a shortage of chips, however, Sony only shipped 500,000 PS2s to the United States, causing a furor, as hard-core gamers sought to get their hands on one of the devices. (Some critics have suggested that it was a marketing ploy by Sony to whip up demand for the PS2s.) Sony has also several dozen video games for the PlayStation II now and another fifty are being created by various game makers.

To see the difference between the new consoles and the old ones, consider the following: the earlier 64-bit consoles could generate 250 polygons (elements in a wire mesh figures used to create three dimensional human figures) to create a character and the new PlayStation II can generate 66 million polygons to create a character. It is obvious that these new generation consoles represent an enormous improve ment, in terms of detail that is possible in generating characters, over earlier ones.

Sega's hope to have "stolen the market" by the time the competing video game consoles by Sony and Nintendo came out hasn't happened, but the Dreamcast has been quite successful. Despite the fact that the Sega has had impressive sales in the United States when its Dreamcast first came on the market, it still only has a relatively small percentage of the game console market. Sega has sold an estimated five million consoles since Dreamcast was introduced, but this is a relatively small percentage of the world market. In all of these new machines, the images are similar in quality to what is found in animated movies. The difference between animated movies and video games, of course, is that video games are interactive and allow the players to manipulate the animated figures in the games.

The outdated Sega (that is pre-Dreamcast) and Nintendo video game consoles in the United States still use a relatively "puny" 64-bit processor, which are only half as powerful as the new Sega Dreamcast's 128-bit processor. Sega estimates its Dreamcast is fifteen times more powerful than the PlayStation 1, the earlier version of Sony's video game player, and ten times more powerful than Nintendo's current game machine. Sega also introduced a large number of video games at the same time it introduced the Dreamcast, so players wouldn't be frustrated by having a powerful video game player but no games to play on it.

Sony, on the other hand, claims its new PlayStation II is many times more powerful than the new Sega Dreamcast. The capacities of video game players are important because makers of video games manufacturers have to decide which platform to design their games for. At the same time, all-purpose personal computer makers are working to beef up their audio-visual capabilities, to compete—as video game platforms—with Nintendo, Sega, and Sony. And in 2001, Microsoft will introduce its X-Box, a dedicated computer that it will manufacture to compete with Sega, Sony and Nintendo. Microsoft claims the hard-disk drive and graphics capabilities of its X-Box will be three times faster than the new Sony PS2 and the forthcoming Nintendo GameCube. Video game consoles currently don't have hard drives, so the X-Box will be quite different from the traditional consoles. Whether game players will be willing to wait until 2001 for the X-Box remains to be seen.

Microsoft decided to compete with Sony when it announced the capabilities of its PlayStation 2—namely that it would have a DVD drive and a port that will enable it to access the Internet. Microsoft saw the PlayStation 2 as a "Trojan horse" that would put Sony in living rooms and eventually replace conventional computers as the center of home entertainment. And when Microsoft couldn't convince computer manufacturers to manufacture the X-Box, Microsoft decided to hire someone and have them manufacture it for them. It is going to use a newly developed NVidia chip, which runs at a trillion operations a second; that is three times faster than the Sony chip in its PlayStation 2.

The fact that Microsoft is getting into the video game console business suggests that video games have attained a degree of acceptance that few would have imagined five or ten years ago. Once thought of as simple little games, like *Pong,* video games have now emerged as a major art form—one that is best played on consoles with graphics capacities approximating super-powerful computers such as those manufactured by Silicon Graphics—computers that cost twenty times as much as the video game consoles do.

There is, we can see, a great deal of competition among console makers and personal computer makes to serve as platforms for video games. Personal computer makers are also developing new and rather expensive boards that greatly increase their power and their ability to generate realistic images and striking audio. Quite obviously, the presence in millions of living rooms of powerful little boxes that allow people to play video games, see DVDs, and cruise the Internet, represents a challenge to computer and software manufacturers. They can only wonder—what will these inexpensive mini-supercomputers be able to do next?

Many industry analysts suggest that Sega's future rests on the success of the Dreamcast console. If it sells enough consoles and attains "critical mass," video game makers will produce games for it and it can prosper. If it doesn't, the company may not survive. It takes around eighteen months to create a video game and the costs of making video games have been rising between 30 percent and 40 percent for the new generations of video games, so the power of the console and the way game developers respond to it are very important.

In the chart below, I compare the various video game playing devices.

Company	Sega	Sony	Nintendo	Microsoft
Device	Dreamcast	PlayStation 2	Game-Cube	X-Box
Chip Speed	200 mhz	295 mhz	405 mhz	733 mhz
Price	$199	$299	?	$300
Online Gaming	Yes	Probably	Yes	Yes
Games	200	52*	?	20?
DVD Player	No	Yes	No	Yes
Released on	Sept. 1999	Oct. 2000	Oct. 2001	?Fall 2001?

* 800 PlayStation 1 Games are also available

We can see there are considerable differences in the design of the various competing game playing consoles. In the final analysis, the most important things for gamers are how well the consoles play video games and how good the video games are. It is also possible to play many video games on computers, but it can be more expensive to purchase special boards to more fully utilize the video and audio capabilities of video games than to purchase a separate console, such as the Sony PlayStation 2.

The Cost of Video Game Playing

There are a number of devices that players can purchase to use with their consoles. Let's consider the Dreamcast which has Dreamcast Controllers" ($29.95), "Dreamcast Racing Wheels" ($38.95), "Dreamcast Fighter Sticks" ($38.95), and various games that cost between $40 and $50 per game.

You can see that there is a considerable investment required to play console video games. Personal Computer versions of video games are often less expensive and, of course, don't require the investment of several hundred dollars in the video console. But dedicated gamers often purchase expensive cards that cost hundreds of dollars, to make their computers better suited for playing games.

Let's take a typical situation and see what it costs to be a gamer as of the beginning of 2000 AD.

$199	console (Sega Dreamcast)
$60	two Dreamcast controllers
$200	four or five Dreamcast video games
$459	*Total*

Older versions of video games are often discounted considerably and used games are available at many video game stores—but gamers don't seem to be terribly concerned about waiting for bargains and saving money. It is unlikely, also, that a gamer will be content with just four games. If a gamer buys ten games over the course of a year, we're now talking about between $400 and $500 a year for just video games. For $500 a person can go to more than sixty movies at $8.00 per ticket, so in terms of one's yearly entertainment budget, video games can be quite significant.

The statistics on relative penetration of the United States video console market are, in approximate figures:

Sony	60 percent
Nintendo	30 percent
Sega	5 percent

As I mentioned earlier, Sony is selling these consoles at a loss in Japan (that may reach as much as $180 a PlayStation there) but will make enormous amounts of money on licensing the games (Sony makes game designers pay a licensing fee to use its platform) and the sales of the games, assuming they are successful, that is. It only costs around $6.00 to manufacture a game cartridge, once a game has been designed, and it will cost even less to manufacture a CD-ROM or DVD disk with a game on it. Manufacturers of video game consoles are willing to lose money on their consoles because they know that once someone has purchased their console, they have to buy video games that use them—and the video games are where the money is.

What will happen when the PlayStation II, the Sega Dreamcast, the new Nintendo Game-Cube, and the Microsoft X-Box slug it out for the hearts and pocketbooks of game players in 2001 might be even more exciting than any video games these corporations produce.

Although Sega has sold five million Dreamcasts a short while ago, it looked like it might be marginalized and even go out of business. Its future is still somewhat shaky which has made some serious game players decide to buy the new Sony PlayStation 2 or wait for the new Nintendo Game-Cube or Microsoft X-Box in 2001.

The Size of the Video Game Industry

Most people are surprised to find out that the video game industry is larger than the film industry. The Interactive Digital Software Association (IDSA) released figures in 1998 that revealed that the video and computer games industry "generated 16 billion dollars in economic activity in 1997, not including computer and video game hardware sales." In 2000 it is a 20 billion dollar a year industry and is expected to grow considerably.

This figure indicates that the amount of money spent just for the games, on cartridges and CD ROMs, is enormous—and to this you have to add the amount of money spent on the consoles and other hardware. In a different report, the IDSA reports that video games are "the fastest growing entertainment industry in America, surpassing books, records and movie box office" (1998 Executive Summary).

Let me cite some other interesting statistics taken from a variety of IDSA reports—all of which I obtained from its web site HYPERLINK *http://www.idsa.com:*

1. Household penetration of "next generation" video consoles will reach between 27–30 million by 1998. (There are approximately 100 million households in America, which means there will be next generation video consoles in one out of every three households.)
2. It often costs more than three million dollars to produce a video game
3. Almost twice as many people identified PC and video games as being more fun than watching television (34 percent vs. 18 percent), and more than double the number said it was more fun than going out to the movies (34 percent vs. 16 percent).
4. There were almost two interactive games sold for every household in America—that is, approximately 200 million games.
5. Fifty-four percent of those most frequently playing console games and 69 percent of PC gamers are 18 or older and 89 percent of video gamers are purchased by adults.
6. Thirty-five percent of console gamers and more than 43 percent of PC gamers are women.
7. People spent $98 million in 2000 renting video games. The sales growth of video games over the past few years has been rapid as the following figures indicate:

DATE:	1995	1996	1997	1998	1999	2000
BILLIONS	$3.2	$3.7	$4.4	$5.5	$6.1	$6.0

Video games greatly outpaced other forms of entertainment in 1998 in terms of growth:

ITEM	Books	Records	Films	Video Games
GROWTH	6.4 percent	5.7 percent	9.2 percent	25 percent

These statistics reveal that the video game industry is very large and growing even larger and very rapidly. We find that most gamers are adults, eighteen and over, and that contrary to what many people believe, a considerable percentage of gamers are women. In a typical year, something like 2,000 new games are introduced. This is the equivalent, we must realize, of more than forty new films opening every week.

We see, also, that there are some differences between PC video game players and console players, in terms of the kinds of video games they prefer. These differences are revealed in the chart the follows, which shows the genres PC and console players prefer in order of preference:

PC Players	**Console**
Puzzle/Board/Card/Learning	Action
Action	Puzzle/Board/Card
Strategy, Driving/Racing/	Driving/Racing
Adventure/Role Playing	Adventure/Role Playing
Sports	Sports
Simulation/ Children's Stories	Strategy
Creativity	Learning
	Children's Stories
	Creativity

As I mentioned earlier, there are often problems in determining the genres of certain video games. Racing games and wrestling games are easy to classify, but others, which involve role playing, are more difficult to classify as belonging to one particular genre. This matter of categorizing games according to their genres is similar to the problems literary scholars have in categorizing novels and other works of fiction; in many cases, a work blends several genres so it isn't easy to pigeonhole a text in just one genre.

The IDSA suggests that the most popular types of games purchased for all platforms are, in order of importance, Action, Sports and Puzzle/ Board/Card Games. There also are many online Internet games that have become popular. People who play these games average three hours a week online and another 5.4 hours playing offline games on their PCs, for a total of 8.4 hours a week playing video games. That is, relatively speaking, a considerable investment of time in playing video games.

The Historical Development of Video Games

Modern video games can be said to have started with graphics-based games such as *Pong, Donkey Kong, Battle Zone, Centipede, Asteroids, Missile Command, Space Invaders* and *Pac-Man*—in the early 1980s. *Pong* was created in 1972 and was a relatively primitive game, that approximated Ping-Pong, but *Pac-Man,* created in 1980, represented a major leap forward as far as the design of video games was concerned. It started as an arcade game and was very popular, so a home version was designed, that was enormously successful. There was also a *Ms. Pac-Man,* which appealed to many female players. *Pac-Man* was the most popular video game in America for several years.

The game players or consoles that people use to play video games are devices designed to generate sharp video images, complex animated characters and powerful sound effects. The arcade version of *Pac-Man* had eighty-four circuit chips on its central logic board and was, for the times, a very powerful device. The first home version was a good deal less powerful and for many gamers, not as satisfying, but Atari, which manufactured the games, added special microprocessors devoted to generating better video displays and sounds. These versions were more satisfying to video game enthusiasts.

From this relatively simple game, played on a maze, that featured monsters gobbling up dots, the video game industry has progressed to its current stage in which there are incredibly complex stories with graphics and sound that now rival those found in animated films. The changes that have taken place from *Pong* and *Pac-Man* to *Myst, Riven, Tomb Raider (*featuring a voluptuous heroine named *Lara Croft*) and *Half-Life* have been truly startling.

The software for some early video games could fit on a 3.25-inch diskette. For example, an early version of *Prince of Persia* fits on a 3.25-inch diskette. The difference between the amount of data stored on a 3.25-inch diskette and a CD-ROM is quite incredible; a CD-ROM contains more than 500 times as much data as a 3.25-inch diskette, which explains why contemporary video games have such powerful images and sound (music and sound effects). The technology involved in creating and playing these games has improved enormously in just a few decades. Most personal computers, for example, are still (as of the year 2000) in the 32-bit mode, so the new Sony and Nintendo consoles, as I pointed out earlier, will be 128-bits and much more powerful machines.

2

Narratives in the Electronic Age

> *"As a format for electronic narrative, the maze is a more active version of the immersive visit. . . . Maze-based stories take away the moving platform and turn the passively observant visitor into a protagonist who must find his or her own way through the fun house. A typical maze-based puzzle game sends you, the player, through a multitiered space vaguely resembling an* Arabian Nights *palace. You operate an avatar who walks through the palace rooms, whose tiled floors and ornately decorated corners often hide treasures that are tricky to perceive. . . . The game is like a treasure hunt in which a chain of discoveries acts as a kind of Ariadne's thread to lead you through the maze to the treasure at the center."*
> —Janet H. Murray (1997: 130–31)

In this chapter I deal with storytelling and how it has changed as it has moved from print to electronic media. I will also consider a number of different aspects of the video game industry as it relates to video games for children. I will deal with the following topics:

1. The media in which children's stories were found before the widespread popularity of computers and game players;
2. The similarities and differences between print and interactive narratives;
3. The uses and gratifications provided by print narratives and video games; and
4. The future of print narratives in a digital age.

There are both print and image-based interactive narratives and video games but since I'm dealing with media for children, I will confine my attention to image-based ones—the ones children of various ages read/ play. Before the development of interactive fictions and video games, mass-mediated children's narratives were found in both print and electronic form:

Print	**Electronic**
Newspapers (Comics Strips)	Radio
Comic Books	Television
Books	Films
Magazines	Records and Videos
Visual & Linear	*Audio-Visual & Linear*

The development of computers and game playing devices by Nintendo, Sony and Sega, led to an enormous growth in the popularity of interactive, non-linear video games and to a new development in children's literature and entertainment—interactive websites. On these websites we generally find simple games and stories for children and some educational content. (I might point out that the definitions of the terms interactive, non-linear, text, narrative and game are subjects of considerable debate among scholars.)

We can deal with stories and narratives along two axes:

1. the media in which they are found and
2. their degree of linearity or non-linearity.

I propose, since there is some question about how linear print texts are and how non-linear electronic ones are, we substitute strong linearity and weak linearity for linear and non-linear. The figure below shows how I see media lining up relative to strong and weak linearity.

I will not be dealing with comic strips or comic books, or stories found in magazines designed for children, which are important media for carrying stories that children read and like. My focus here will be on the "traditional" book and the new media, such as video games and video fictions.

I might add that although I tend to focus upon video games for children, my comments also apply to video games in general.

FIGURE 2.1

Linearity

		+*Strong*	*Weak—*
Electronic Audio-Visual		Film TV Radio	Music **Video Games** Videos MTV Avant Garde Films, Videos
Medium			
Print		**Children's Books** Comic Strips Stories in Magazines	Postmodern Novels, Plays, etc.

A Set of Bipolar Oppositions Between Print and Electronic Narratives

I will begin by offering a set of bipolar oppositions that can be made in comparing interactive and print narratives, keeping in mind that this list is simplistic and some oppositions have been, shall we say, "forced" into place. What this list of oppositions does is enable us to see how stories in found these two media—print and interactive electronic ones on the Internet, game players and CD-ROMs—differ. Print and electronic narratives also are similar, in certain important respects, which I will discuss later. I will be confining my discussion to texts with a narrative dimension to them, and thus excluding a number of genres of video games.

What this table does is map out, in a rather extreme way, the differences between printed narratives—that is, books, and electronic narratives and video games. The difference between print narratives and electronic ones is, let me suggest, found not so much in the *histoire* (what happens) but in the *discours* (the way the histoire is expressed) . . . or more correctly the media-discourse.

Let me discuss a few of these polarities. Printed narratives are linear, in that they are made up of lines of print and this linearity suggests, as McLuhan has explained, rationality and logical thinking.

TABLE 2.2
Differences Between Print and Electronic Interactive Narratives

Print Narratives (Books)	Electronic Narratives
1. Linear & Multi-Linear	Non-Linear/ Multi-directional
2. Author tells, Reader "Listens"	"Reader/Player" is part of story
3. Author is Creative but	Designer is "Creative" but
(Role of Reader great)	(Role of Player great)
4. Hot Medium (McLuhan)	Cool Medium (McLuhan)
Low in Participation	High in Participation
5. Words basic	Visual images and sound basic
6. Reader guided through territory	Reader/Player explores territory
7. Interior world basic	Exterior world basic
8. Imagination	Immersion
9. Strong characterization	Weak characterization
10. Endings Strong	Endings Weak or problematical
11. Reader external to events	Reader/Player is Internal to events
12. Participation by identification	Actual participation
13. Characters have great freedom	Characters select from available choices
14. Illustrations relatively simple	Graphics, Music and Sound Powerful
15. Construction of story hidden	Construction of story discovered
16. Many kinds of structure	Mazes & Tangled Rhizomes (Murray)
17. Human Relations basic	Achieving goals basic
18. Willing suspension of disbelief	Activity leads to involvement

With the development of reader response theory, we can argue that readers—children and adults—play an important part in print stories and based on their backgrounds and interests, "read" stories actively. Everyone reads stories differently, so it isn't accurate to assume that everyone gets the same message from printed narratives or that the experience is as linear as one might imagine.

That is, when people read a printed text, they often relate to it in what might be thought of as an interactive manner. People can look at the end of a book to see how it comes out or reread sections of it, and they read books dialogically and intertextually—thinking about what they read in terms of other information they have and other texts they have read. Our minds often wander when we read and that can be seen as a kind of interactivity—as printed matter generates fantasies, day-dreams, and similar types of behavior. I think that video games don't have the same power to generate fantasies because the player is so actively involved in the game and the images are so powerful that they tend to preclude the kind of fantasizing books facilitate.

There are some books, also, that are designed to be interactive; you can start at various places, skip around in the text and take other actions that affect the way you "read" the book. As Roland Barthes explains in *The Pleasure of the Text*,

> Thus, what I enjoy in a narrative is not directly its content or structure, but rather the abrasions I impose upon the fine surface: I read on, I skip, I look up, I dip in again. Which has nothing to do with the deep laceration the text of bliss inflicts upon language itself, and not upon the simple temporality of its reading. (1975: 11–12)

When they read books, children also often skip around, so book reading isn't always linear. In electronic interactive narratives, the role of the reader/player is, in many cases, quite limited—it involves finding and choosing from various links that are available. These links provide information or impact upon the narrative itself in various ways. In video games, players can often make choices about the powers and attributes various characters will have and these choices affect what happens in the game. From what I can gather, the more narrative structure an interactive narrative has, the less impact readers/players have on the eventual outcome of the story. The less plot it has, the greater the impact of reader/player choices. It seems that random access and narrative pleasure don't always go together.

McLuhan has suggested that electronic media are extensions of our central nervous systems and are "cool," offering relatively little data, which leads to a greater sense of participation. Print media, McLuhan argues, are "hot" and offer a great deal of data, which engenders low participation. That might explain the fascination that people have with these electronic media and the passion with which they become involved in them. From McLuhan's perspective, the video screen, with its millions of dots, offers less data than print does. On the other hand, the fact that readers of books become powerfully involved in the world and the characters created by the writer must be kept in mind.

With print narratives, readers use their imaginations to become involved in the texts. With electronic narratives, readers/players become "immersed" in the texts. They do this usually by manipulating *avatars* (virtual constructs that are controlled by human players and function as a means of interacting with other people or characters) or cursors, symbols that represent the screen position of some pointing device and that often change in shape to indicate their function at any moment. I don't believe that these two devices for representing characters provides the richness that characters in printed texts have, though it can be argued that the lack of interiority in interactive texts actually helps generate reader/player immersion. This immersion is also intensified by the use of stunning audio-visual techniques (lighting, sound effects, and music) in many interactive texts.

How Interactive Narratives and Print Narratives are Similar

First, and this is of considerable importance, both video games/ electronic narratives and printed stories (and orally told stories, as well) involve what Vladimir Propp, author of *Morphology of the Folktale,* would describe as a narrative line with "functions." A function can be defined as any activity of a character that has some impact on the events in the text. Propp puts is this way, "Function is understood as an act of a character, defined from the point of view of its significance for the course of the action" (1968:21).

This definition is very similar to the one Brenda Laurel gives for functionality in programs in computer games, *"the actions that are performed by people and computers working in concert, and programs are the means for creating the potential for those actions"* (1991:45). The reason for this similarity is that both Propp and Laurel and dealing with stories, and in stories, as Propp reminds us, "the functions of the dramatis personae are basic components of the tale" and "an action cannot be defined apart from its place in the course of narration" (1968:21).

In the final analysis, narratives have sequences of actions that lead to some kind of a resolution. In technical terms, we would say that narratives have a *syntagmatic* structure—a sequence of events that are linked, in various ways, to one another. Propp's book is considered a classic and, I would suggest, still is useful even though it was written many years ago.

His thirty-one functions (listed in the appendix), in various permutations, combinations, modernizations, and postmodernizations, are, it can be argued, at the heart of all narratives—not just the Russian folktales Propp analyzed in obtaining his list. That means they inform all our print stories and all our electronic interactive ones, though in the electronic narratives situations may be a good deal more complicated. (This might explain, in part, why video games from Japan are so popular in America and why American films are so popular all over the world.)

There are, for Propp, two kinds of heroes: *victim heroes* (who suffer from the acts of a villain and have to redeem themselves) and *seeker heroes* (who are sent off to accomplish some goal). Nowadays, of course, we would have to add victim and seeker *heroines,* like Lara Croft, to Propp's list. Both victim and seeker heroes and heroines have to go places—either to redeem themselves or to find whatever it is they are seeking.

We might term these Proppian functions "narratemes," the essential building blocks of all stories. If Propp is right, and there are only a limited number of functions or narratemes found in narratives, then the most important difference between print narratives and electronic narratives discussed in the polarities listed above involve the ways in which electronic narratives make the "reader" or "player" into one of the characters involved in the story and give readers/players a sense of agency. This sense of agency is restricted, or perhaps illusory is more accurate, since players often only have a limited number of actions they can choose, though their activities do influence what happens in a story.

Interactive Narratives and Interactive Video Games

I would describe the following genres of video games as the most important ones:

1. Simulations
2. Real-Time Strategy Games
3. First Person Shooters
4. Action-Arcade Games
5. Adventure Games
6. Role Playing Games (RPGs)
7. Sports Games

Some of these genres, like Action-Arcade Games (wrestling games, *Mortal Kombat,* etc.) have relatively little narrative content but others, like Adventure Games (*Tomb Raider, Myst, Riven, The Oregon Trail, Where in the World is Carmen Sandiego?*), have a considerable amount of narrative content. But things happen in games of all kinds and I think we can portray these things that happen as having a quasi-narrative dimension to them. There are also mixed genre narratives and video games as well. Some critics describe *Tomb Raider* as a mixed genre adventure-shooter narrative.

TABLE 2.3
Similarities Between Games and Stories

Interactive Video Games	Interactive Narratives
Often like a story	Often like a game
Player is "hero" of game	Hero is "player" in story
Contest basic	Conflict basic
Winners and Losers	Heroes win, Villains lose
Chance	Chance and courage: moral elements
Intelligence in strategizing	Intelligence in finding clues, etc.
Active participants	Active reader

It is at the extremes that we find the most significant differences between interactive narratives and video games. That is, both electronic narratives and several important genres of video games share many things, which I've outlined in the chart below. We live in an age of blended genres and it is not stretching things too much to suggest that many stories have "contest" elements in them just as many games have "narrative" elements in them. It's hard to say whether some video games are games or really stories with game elements in them. Of course, there are some games, like flight simulation games and first-person shooter games that have little narrative content. But others, like adventure games (which generally are played on computers) and role-playing games have considerable narrative content. Let me explain how I arrived at this conclusion by comparing and contrasting video games and interactive stories "in general."

We can see, then, that there are a number of similarities that exist between some video games and electronic interactive stories. I've seen some scholars write about "narrative video games," as a matter of fact. Henry Jenkins discusses video games as narratives in his dialogue with Mary Fuller in "Nintendo and New World Travel Writing: A Dialogue" (quoted in Steven G. Jones, [ed.] *Cybersociety: Computer-Mediated Communication and Community,* Sage Publications, 1995) and argues "Most of the criteria by which we might judge a classically constructed narrative fall by the wayside when we look at these games as storytelling systems" (1995:61). He points out, taking a cue from De Certeau, that spatial relations are a central aspect of narratives:

Although plot structures (kidnapping and rescue, pursuit and capture, street fighting, invasion and defense) are highly repetitive . . . what never loses its interest in video games is the promise of moving into the next space, of mastering these worlds and making them your own playground. So although the child's play is framed by narrative logic, it remains largely uncontrolled by plot dictates. (1995: 62)

The plots in many electronic narratives may be elemental and thin, but that doesn't prevent them from appealing to people reading/playing them. There is reason to suggest that the more defined the narrative and the characters, the less room there is for the child to imagine things and perhaps even enjoy the game. Also, the intertextual aspects of some games means that characters have highly defined personalities that they carry over from some medium—such as the comics—to the game.

In *The Semiotic Challenge*, Roland Barthes reminds us of Aristotle's views about characters:

In Aristotelian poetics, the notion of character is secondary, entirely subsidiary to the notion of action: there can be stories without "characters," Aristotle says; there cannot be characters without a story. (1988: 109)

I don't see how one can have a story without any characters in it, I must confess. It may be that interactive narratives and action-adventure computer games, are narratives in which action is dominant and characterization is of secondary importance or maybe even irrelevant. Aristotle would approve of video games, it would seem! Propp would not!

These games/stories maintain narrative interest by providing new territories to conquer with new challenges and new characters with whom to interact. Michel de Certeau has written in *The Practice of Everyday Life*,

... narrative structures have the status of spatial syntaxes. By means of a whole panoply of codes, ordered ways of proceeding and constraints, they regulate changes in space (or moves from one place to another) made by stories in the forms of places put in linear or interlaced series: from here (Paris), one goes there (Montargis); this place (a room) includes another (a dream or memory); etc. (1984: 115)

It may be that the spatial explorations in print narratives, video games and interactive narratives are more important than the interiority of the central characters? I don't know how much "interiority" young children are looking for when they play games or "read" electronic narratives. They may not be looking for character development and interiority in print books, either.

As one person I interviewed at Lucas Learning explained to me, "kids want to play games. They want heroes, villains and magic." Those items, found in games, are also, let me suggest, found in narratives—electronic and print, as we shall see.

Adventure video games are slightly more popular than violent video games. According to data from PC Data, cited by Stephen C. Miller in the *New York Times* (July 29, 1999, page D3) two adventure games, *Myst* and *Riven*, had combined sales of 5.5 million copies as contrasted to violent games such as *Doom* and *Quake* that had combined sales of 4.7 million copies. Although there are many different genres of video games, it seems that adventure video games, which have a strong narrative component, are one of the most important categories or genres of video games.

The Medium of the Message and the Massage

I have suggested that print narratives and interactive narratives have essentially the same narrative structures. That is, both employ Propp's functions. What's different is that in electronic narratives, the player gains agency—takes on the role of the hero or heroine and participates in the action. Maybe McLuhan was right—the medium *is* the message, by which he meant that the texts carried by the medium are less important than the attributes and implications of the medium itself.

In his book *The Medium is the Massage,* McLuhan explains his position:

> The alphabet and print technology fostered and encouraged a fragmenting process, a process of specialism and detachment. Electric technology fosters and encourages unification and involvement . . . Youth instinctively understands the present environment—the electric drama. It lives mythically and in depth. This is the reason for the great alienation between generations. (1967: 8, 9)

McLuhan argued, also, that each medium is an extension of some human faculty. Books, he said, are extensions of the eye while electronic media are extensions of our central nervous systems. Different media change our sense perceptions, which means that the extension of one sense alters our other senses and the way we perceive the world.

Electronic media are, McLuhan suggested, forcing us to live in a global village where everyone is interconnected and everything happens "all at once." I wonder whether this global village can be used as a metaphor for the landscapes that have to be explored in so many video games/electronic narratives. They are mythic and they involve players in depth. It almost sounds, at times, as if McLuhan is describing video games in *The Medium is the Massage*. McLuhan's ideas also imply, I would suggest, a sexual masturbatory element to game playing with its joysticks or other kinds of extensions of ourselves.

Your Next Adventure

In "Interactive Entertainment: Who writes it? Who reads It? Who needs It?" (*Wired*, September 1995), Charles Platt offers an interesting insight into interactive stories. He points out that interactive stories are written in the second person, with "you" taking on the role of the main character:

> This second person storytelling form is unique to interactive entertainment. It has hardly even been used elsewhere. To understand why, consider a conventional story based around that age-old plot device, the romantic triangle. [He then describes a typical romantic triangle in which a married woman becomes involved with a single man.] The way this situation develops will depend entirely on the personalities of the characters. This is how fiction works: the writer creates characters, and the characters carry the story. Now suppose that story becomes interactive. In other words, the reader is allowed to control the story. This means that the characters have been robbed of their most important function. They have become pawns who do whatever they are told. How can the reader respect them or believe in them anymore? (1995: 146, 147)

This creates serious problems, Platt suggests. The only way to solve them is to have the central character become "generic" and simple, so it fits as many readers as possible.

We end up, inevitably, Platt argues, with "simplified heroes with very basic motives: to find a reward and avoid getting killed. As a result, the product feels more like a game than a real story." That's why, Platt argues, there have been no interactive fictions that have attracted an adult audience. Children and adolescents might like interactive fictions, because they can have some control over the narrative, but there is something in the nature of the interactive beast that prevents these stories from appealing to adults. The solution, Platt suggests, is to get rid of storytelling, and let people who create interactive stories ignore plots and just create a good illusion of reality and let people play around in it.

TABLE 2.4
Uses and Gratifications in Print and Electronic Games

Print Uses & Gratifications	Electronic Uses & Gratifications
To amuse oneself and be amused.	To amuse oneself and be amused
To satisfy curiosity and be informed.	To satisfy curiosity and be informed
To reinforce a belief in justice	*To struggle to achieve justice*
To obtain an outlet for drives	To obtain an outlet for drives
To socialize, have relationships with others	To socialize, have relationships with others
To read about magic and the marvelous	*To experience magic and the marvelous*
To learn about history	*To be involved in historical events*
To see villains in action	*To battle against villains*
To find models to imitate.	*To imitate models*

Although video games may start off with a second person "you" command, it seems to me that they quickly shift into a first person "I" or "we" (if one is involved in a team of heroes and heroines) as the player becomes immersed in the game. The player identifies with his or her character. For example, in *Riven,* at the start of the adventure the player/reader is told "you must rescue Catherine, etc., etc.). When I play *Riven*, I always feel that I am the presence behind the cursor, investigating this fantastic world.

Uses and Gratifications of Electronic Narratives

The "uses and gratifications" school of media analysis asks what benefits people get from media rather than what effects the media have on them. I will list a number of uses and gratifications that these electronic narratives offer. Many of them also are found in printed texts, except that printed texts do not provide the gratifications that come from agency because readers don't "act" but participate vicariously in actions.

Most of the uses (to which people put narratives) and gratifications (which people get from narratives) apply to both interactive and print texts, but a few of them involve more direct participation by the reader/ player. Thus, for example, video games allow the reader to actually battle against villains while print narratives require the reader to imagine doing so. I have put these interactive uses and gratifications in italics to highlight them. Personally speaking, I think using one's imagination and envisioning heroes, heroines, villains, magical kingdoms, and so on is often a more powerful and interesting than manipulating an avatar but many children don't seem to agree with me.

Will Interactive Narratives Replace Print Narratives?

Some writers have suggested that video games and electronic narratives will eventually be hard to distinguish from television programs and films. Right now they seem to be at the animated comic strip and cartoon or perhaps graphic novel stage of development, often with beautiful renderings of landscapes and people and superb music and sound effects.

But we know that game players are becoming increasingly more powerful and able to handle more advanced electronics. If electronic narratives "evolve" and become indistinguishable from television shows and films, except that we don't read them or just look at them but play roles in them, it will mean that people will no longer just have the fifteen minutes of fame that has been allotted to them. They will now have twenty or forty hours of stardom, playing certain roles, in interactive stories they purchase, a kind of interactive dramatic elaboration of the karaoke experience.

If that's where things are heading, then I would argue that the printed narratives found in books will still be the best source of entertainment and instruction for children, as well as the old and the not-so-old. The interaction that takes place between the mind of a reader and that of the writer (and perhaps the unconscious of both as well) will be better than the interaction we get from video games.

This means that children will still find joy and pleasure in printed books and though, when they are not watching television, they will probably devote a good deal of their time to video games and electronic narratives, printed books will not become irrelevant in their lives. And that is because as powerful and remarkable as images are and can be, they still can't compete with our imaginations and the "willing suspension of belief" books provide.

We go to fictive narratives in all media to escape from ourselves, to gain insights from other people, to experience other worlds. De Certeau has written (1984:169), "To write is to produce the text; to read is to receive it from someone else without putting one's mark on it, without remaking it." The more we contribute to a narrative, I would suggest, the less we can escape into the world an author of a narrative creates and the less satisfying the experience is. Children will continue to play video games and read/play interactive narratives, but I can't imagine that they will give up the lasting pleasure of the text (that is, the printed text) for the momentary and transitory excitement of the video image.

An Ironic Situation: Video Games as Aids to Reading Books

It may even be that playing interactive narratives will lead to more book reading!

As David F. Lancy and Bernard L. Hayes have argued in "Interactive Fiction and the Reluctant Reader" (Nov., 1988 *English Journal, 42*):

> The "genre" is characterized by combining sophisticated programming with traditional tools of the storyteller to create engrossing fictional worlds. Some people maintain that interactive fiction, even in its infancy, marks a new literary form. These claims are debatable, but there is no doubt that these sophisticated interactive games involve the reader in activities that clearly require and enhance behaviors that many current reading theorists would emphasize as important and essential in developing reading comprehension strategies.

The authors discovered that students who hardly ever read spent as much as three hours a day in reading activities while involved with interactive texts and concluded that

> students with no more than average interest in reading will spend a great amount of time engaged in interactive fiction that requires quite a lot of reading if they are successful at the quest. We view this as having important implications for encouraging students to read independently. (1988: 45)

There is reason to suggest, then, that interactive fictions and adventure games that have strong narrative components will not replace book reading but may actually stimulate it. Television viewing will probably suffer from this, but rescuing young people from this "vast wasteland" is, I believe, something to be desired.

Conclusions and Questions to Think About

We live in a postmodern age and it would seem that our video games and interactive narratives are the kinds of entertainments that most closely reflect the postmodern ethos. The barriers that used to exist between elite arts and popular culture have been battered down; the role of the reader and the author are now merging and authors no longer have the same status they had. But even in a postmodern digital age, with its video digi-narratives, endless web sites devoted to inter-active narratives, games, and the like, certain gratifications that chil-dren seek from their entertainments are still, I would say, best served by the printed book.

The possibilities found in video games and interactive fictions are quite incredible. But just as audio enthusiasts find the sound in long playing records to be warmer than the sound in CDs, it seems likely that the written word will continue to have its attractions. It has been said that the written word lives; the written word—that is, the printed word—will continue to live—especially for children, even though they may find electronic narratives wonderful and fascinating.

Many of the new adventure video games are quite remarkable. In one game, for example, there are (so the description of the game on the Internet reads) some fifty-five characters, 7,000 lines of dialogue and ninety exotic locations. Some of these games are quite brilliant and video games, in all genres, will play an important role in enter-taining and educating young (and not so young) children.

The very nature of video games, however, limits their capacity to do certain things—because, I would suggest, once again, what we create in our imaginations is infinitely greater than anything we can create in the form of images in any medium. And though the games and narratives are interactive, they still are stories and have heroes and heroines who are sent on missions, have tasks to do, need helpers and magic agents—just like the characters described by Propp in his study of Russian fairy tales.

There is reason to believe, also, that these games cannot take care of the needs of young children the way, for example, fairy tales can. Bruno Bettelheim has been eloquent on this matter in his *The Uses of Enchantment.* And, I would suggest, these video games cannot and never will be able to generate the enchantment and the magic of books like *Treasure Island* or *Alice in Wonderland* or *Swiss Family Robinson* or any other of the great children's literary classics. Immersion and agency cannot compete with imagination. Video games and narratives are also expensive and beyond the reach of millions of children who grow up in societies on the other side of what we now call "the digital divide."

I will pose some questions about these games and children that are, I believe, worth thinking about:

1. Are video games theatrical rather than dramatic? That is, can we say that their appeal basically comes from special effects and "flash" and from providing children with a sense of agency in a game/story rather than from being offered a good story?
2. Do children and others who play these games get an illusory sense of empowerment, a version of "infantile omnipotence," which will be harmful when they get older? I call this "*post-infantile omnipotence.*"
3. Should children (and adults) who are addicted to video games best be thought of as *servo-proteins*—humans who have, in a sense, been "captured" and enslaved by video game players and other electro-mechanical devices? Is there a kind of electronic imperative that draws people to these games? If so, what will happen when electronic "feelies" arrive? Are video games training children to take their place as servants to machines in the new information society?
4. Do many video games, like certain television narratives, expose children to material that is too adult for them. Children cannot read stories that have this kind of adult material in them, because it is too difficult for them, but they can see stories with this material on television and now become involved in such stories in video games and narratives. What impact will "playing" games that has material that is too adult for them have on their emotional development? Are we destroying the latency period and childhood with these games?

Appendix:
Two Theories of Narrative

The first theorist I will discuss is Vladimir Propp, who studied some Russian fairy tales and came up with what he described as the basic actions found in fairy tales—and, it can be argued, all narratives. The fairy tale serves as a basic model and all stories are constructed of various and varying combinations of his functions. Propp's thirty-one functions are listed in the chart below. (He doesn't consider the initial situation to be a function.) These functions often are paired, and there is generally a logical nature to the way they are used in texts—of all kinds. Propp argued that the sequence of events was inviolable, but we

TABLE 2.4
Propp's Thirty-One Functions

Initial Situation:	Members of family introduced, Hero introduced
1. Absentation:	One of the members of the family absents self.
2. Interdiction:	Interdiction addressed to hero. (Can be reversed)
3. Violation:	Interdiction is violated.
4. Reconnaissance:	The villain makes attempt to get information
5. Delivery:	The villain gets information about his victim.
6. Trickery:	The villain tries to deceive his victim.
7. Complicity	Victim is deceived
8. Villainy	Villain causes harm to a member of a family
8a Lack:	Member of family lacks something, desires something
9. Mediation:	Misfortune made known. Hero dispatched
10. Counteraction:	Hero (Seeker) agrees to counteraction
11. Departure:	Hero leaves home
12. 1st Donor Function:	Hero tested, receives magical agent or helper
13. Hero's Reaction:	Hero reacts to agent or donor
14. Receipt of Agent:	Hero acquires use of magical agent
15. Spatial Change:	Hero led to object of search
16. Struggle:	Hero and villain join in direct combat
17. Branding:	Hero is branded
18. Victory:	Villain is defeated
19. Liquidation:	Initial misfortune or lack is liquidated
20. Return:	Hero returns
21. Pursuit, Chase:	Hero is pursued
22. Rescue:	Hero rescued from pursuit
23. Unrecognized Arrival:	Hero, unrecognized, arrives home or elsewhere
24. Unfounded Claims:	False hero presents unfounded claims
25. Difficult Task:	Difficult task is proposed to hero
26. Solution:	The task is resolved
27. Recognition:	The hero is recognized
28. Exposure:	The false hero or villain is exposed
29. Transfiguration:	The hero is given a new appearance
30. Punishment:	The villain is punished
31. Wedding:	The hero is married, ascends the throne

don't need to accept that notion to benefit from his structural analysis of narrative texts. [This chart is from *Narratives in Popular Culture, Media, and Everyday Life* (Sage Publications).]

According to Propp, there are two kinds of heroes: victim heroes and seeker heroes (who are sent on missions to accomplish something). With victim heroes, the focus is on what happens to him and how he ends his victimization. With seeker heroes, the focus is on the way he helps others who have suffered from some kind of villainy or are in danger. Heroes often have helpers who aid them in various ways—they have special powers or they give the hero some kind of magic agent that enables him to prevail over villains. If Propp is correct, all the heroes in video games are either seeker heroes or victim heroes. Quite obviously, many of the heroes and heroines in video games are sent on missions to accomplish some goal. These video games, then, are more modern versions of fairy tales and we can find the same Proppian functions in them, though in modernized versions.

Ronald B. Tobias, another narrative theorist, says there are twenty master plots that all stories draw upon. One reason for this is that there are only certain things that interest us, that can make us become involved in games or stories. In her book, *Hamlet on the Holodeck,* Janet Murray offers a list of Tobias' plots. (I have numbered them and put them in alphabetical order [1997: 186,187]):

1.	Adventure	11.	Quest
2.	Ascension	12.	Rescue
3.	Descension	13.	Revenge
4.	Discovery	14.	Rivalry
5.	Escape	15.	Sacrifice
6.	Forbidden Love	16.	Temptation
7.	Love	17.	The Riddle
8.	Maturation	18.	Transformation
9.	Metamorphosis	19.	Underdog
10.	Pursuit	20.	Wretched Excess

As Murray writes,

> One would be hard put to name any story that did not belong, at least in part, to one of these categories, whether it is *The Incredible Hulk* (metamorphosis), *King Lear* (decension), or *Seinfeld* (refused maturation). These patterns are constant because human experience is constant, and though cultural differences may inflect these patterns differently from one place to another and one historical period to another, the basic events out of which we tell stories are the same for all of us. (1997: 187)

These twenty master plots are another way of making sense of narratives, but I don't think they are as useful as Propp's since they don't enable us to analyze narratives is as much detail as his system does. There are many other narrative theorists who have developed systems for analyzing narratives or who have written on narrative theory, whose work is discussed in my book on narratives.

3

Video Games as Cultural Indicators

> *"Until recently, video games as media forms stood by themselves. They did not create other forms of media. If anything, they were derivative or supplementary. Thus, the movie* RoboCop *spawned the video game of the same name. Now video games create the foundation for new films. This shift is an extremely important one. It suggests that video games have a greater narrative authority than was the case a few years ago—one that is primary rather than derivative compared to other competing media such as film."*
> —Eugene F. Provenzo, Jr. (1997:103)

I would like to explore the cultural significance of video games by examining a number of them in terms of the way that they reflect beliefs and values. These "reflections" are often hidden and have to be teased out of the games. Writers don't generally think about the way the works they create reflect beliefs and values, but it is only natural to assume that one way or another, texts of all kinds—whether they be novels or short stories or films or video games—reflect interesting things about the personalities and beliefs of those who create them and the societies in which they are created.

Avoiding Cognitive Dissonance and Seeking Reinforcement

It is reasonable to assume, then, that video games (and all texts) reflect something about their creators and also about their audiences. We can assume that members of audiences wish to avoid, to the extent they can, *cognitive dissonance*—some kind of a gap between what individuals like and believe and the values found in video games and other texts that they watch or purchase. For example, a person who believes in the self-made man and woman and in individualism would probably find it difficult, if not unpleasant, to play a game in which the basic values are egalitarian and focused on the needs of society rather and the obligations of individuals rather than their rights.

In the same light, people seek *reinforcement* for their beliefs and values. Thus, a strong individualist would seek novels that affirmed the importance of individualism (such as the works of Ayn Rand) and avoid novels and other texts that attacked individualism as being self-centered and selfish and stressed, instead, egalitarianism. These values and beliefs are not always obvious and players of video games might not be able to identify why it is that they feel uncomfortable about a particular game, or don't like it, but in many cases there are conflicts in values that are important in generating these feelings.

Let me offer a different analogy and a rather far-fetched example. A person who believes in the Republican political ideology would find it unpleasant to play a video game that reflects the Democratic political ideology. In many cases young people haven't decided what their basic values are, so they can play different video games without being bothered by dissonance.

Analyzing Video Games for Values and Covert Attitudes and Beliefs

When we wish to analyze video games for values and beliefs, we do the same thing we do when analyzing a work of fiction. We look at the following matters:

1. What is the symbolic significance of the heroes, heroines, villains and villainesses.
2. What is the significance of what the characters do? What are their goals?
3. What is posited as "good" and "bad" in the texts?
4. How do the heroes and heroines achieve their goals?
5. What does the ending tell us about beliefs and values?
6. Does the game "teach" players anything about life? If so, what?
7. What concepts and ideas from philosophers, social scientists, and others can we use to make sense of the game?

8. What do the games reflect about matters such as gender, race, age, sex, power, violence, and ethnicity?
9. What motivates the characters? What do these motivations tell us about ourselves?
10. What is the landscape like (or what are the landscapes like) in which the game takes place? What does the setting of the game suggest to us about the societies found in the games?

It is useful to consider the range of video games and the most celebrated examples of each kind of video game. The top forty games, according to a Cnet website *www.gamecenter.com/features/exclusives/ top40* games are, in alphabetical order:

Asteroids (1979)	*Diablo* (1997)
Sid Maier's Civilization II (1996)	*Donkey Kong* (1983)
Combat (1978)	*Doom* (1993)
Defender (1980)	*Dragon's Lair* (1983)
Duke Nukem 3D (1996)	*Quake* (1996)
Final Fantasy (1990)	*Tom Clancy's Rainbow Six* (1998)
Microsoft Flight Sim (1982)	*Resident Evil* (1998)
Gauntlet (1985)	*Sim City* (1987)
Gran Turismo 2 (1992)	*Sonic the Hedgehog* (1989)
Grim Fandango (1998)	*Space Invaders* (1980)
Half-Life (1998)	*Star Wars* (1983)
King's Quest (1983)	*Super Mario Brothers* (1985)
Legend of Zelda (1986)	*System Shock* (1994)
Missile Command (1980)	*Tetrus* (1998)
Mule (1983)	*Ultima IV* (1985)
Myst (1995)	*Virtual Fighter 2* (1995)
Netrek (1989)	*Warcraft II* (1996)
Pac-Man (1980)	*Wing Commander* (1990)
Pitfall (1982)	*X-Com* (1994)
Pong (1972)	*Zork* (1981)

There is another list, of the so-called "50 Best Games Ever!" that *PC Gamer* published in its November 1999 issue. This list, giving the PC games in order of their importance, follows.

1. *Half Life* (1998)
2. *Civilization II* (1996)

3. *Quake I, II* (1996/8)
4. *Star Craft* (1998)
5. *System Shock I, II* (1994/9)
6. *Sid Meier's Alpha Centauri* (1998)
7. *Jedi Knight: Dark Forces II* (1997)
8. *Tie Fighter Collector's CD-ROM* (1995)
9. *X-Com. UFO Defense* (1994)
10. *Heroes of Might & Magic II* (1996)
11. *Tom Clancy's Rainbox Six* (1998)
12. *WarCraft II* (1996)
13. *Baldur's Gate* (1998)
14. C&C: *Red Alert* (1996)
15. Starsiege: *Tribes* (1998)
16. *Links LS 1998 Edition* (1998)
17. *Longbow 2* (1997)
18. *Sam and Max Hit the Road* (1994)
19. *Myth I, II* (1997/9)
20. *Ultima Underworld I, II* (1992)
21. *NHL 98* (1997)
22. *Panzer General II* (1997)
23. *Railroad Tycoon II* (1998)
24. *Red Baron* (1991)
25. *Lemmings* (1991)
26. *Battlezone* (1998)
27. *Alone in the Dark* (1993)
28. *Chuck Yeager's Air Combat* (1993)
29. *Gabriel Knight: Beast Within* (1996)
30. *Duke Nukem 3D* (1996)
31. *Worms: Armageddon* (1999)
32. *Sim City 2000* (1994)
33. *Motorcross Madness* (1998)
34. *Doom* (1993)
35. *Diablo* (1996)
36. *Fallout 1, 2* (1997/98)
37. *Falcon 4.0* (1999)
38. *Curse of Monkey Island* (1998)
39. *High Heat Baseball 2000* (1999)
40. *Ultima VII* (1992)
41. *Unreal* (1998)
42. *Indiana Jones and the Fate of Atlantic* (1992)
43. *Prince of Persia* (1989)
44. *Betrayal at Krondor* (1993)

45. *Master of Orion* (1993)
46. *Thief: the Dark Project* (1998)
47. *FPS Football Pro* (1995)
48. *Tomb Raider* (1996)
49. *You don't Know Jack Huge* (1998)
50. *The Operational Art of War* (1998)

Because the magazine only deals with PC games, it neglected many important games that are played on consoles, but there are still some commonalities between the two lists. Thus, we find on both lists such games as *Civilization II, Diablo, Doom, Duke Nukem, Half-Life* and *System Shock.* The *PC Gamer* list doesn't include some widely admired and influential games such as *Tetrus, Grim Fandango, Myst, Riven, Legend of Zelda,* or *Pac-Man.* Lists such as these are useful because they provide us with a sense of what people in the industry feel are important games, but they are, of course, only opinions. There are also differences in emphasis in the two lists. The gamecenter list is a list of games that are historically important and the second list is a list of "greatest" PC games in terms of their technological and game playing qualities.

Disciplines to Consider When Analyzing Video Games

In my chart on the focal points to consider in analyzing video games, presented in an earlier chapter, I wrote that we can focus our attention on:

1. *Art:*   the game/text/work of art,
2. *Audience*   the audience for the game
3. *America*   the society in which the game is created
4. *Artist*   the artists/writers/musicians who create the game
5. *Medium*   the medium through which the game is transmitted

I would like to suggest, as a further refinement, that we visualize this chart of the focal points with a circle of different academic disciplines deployed around the work of art (that is, the specific video game) and looking at it from their particular point of view. This would look like the chart below:

Scholars from each of these disciplines would see the video game in a different way and each would offer interesting insights into the video game, covering such matters as its appeal, its audience, its ideological messages, the way it communicates meaning (as a system of

FIGURE 3.1
Disciplinary Perspectives on Video Games

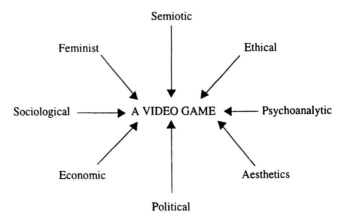

signs), the way it presents women, and its aesthetic qualities. In principle, I would suggest that the best way to analyze any text, whether it is a video game, novel, comic book, painting, or television show is to employ as many of these disciplines as you can to make sense of the text being analyzed. Critics who haven't mastered all of these disciplines can always find critics in a given discipline who have written something useful—either about the text itself or about some concept that will be helpful in analyzing the text. Just as seeker heroes in a video game are sent on some mission, and need helpers to achieve their goals, the same applies with critics. They can use helpers—other critics and scholars who have written material of interest.

4

A Bio-Psycho-Social Perspective
on Video Games

"The contract between user and text in 'interactive fiction' is not merely a 'willing suspension of disbelief' but a willing suspension of one's normal capacity for language, physical aptness and social interaction as well. It is of course not autism in a clinical, or even a fictional sense, but functionally it seems very close.
—Espen J. Aarseth (1997: 116–17)

"We feel confident that we've created very interesting, highly motivating products that will engage and challenge kids. We believe that kids love to learn, especially when they are actively shaping the outcome . . . We want to be sure the basic game play itself is engaging, without all the bells and whistles. Even kids who come to our user testing sessions looking for more "action" (e.g. violence) seem to get hooked on the game play."
—Jane Boston, Lucas Learning, quoted in *T.H.E. Journal.*

Now I would like to offer a bio-psycho-social perspective on the video game phenomenon. This focus on the biological, psychological, and sociological aspects of video games means that I will discuss them in terms of their impact on our physical bodies, our minds or psyches, and our societies. I will start from a biological perspective, recognizing that what happens to our bodies also affects our minds and may have societal effects as well.

A Biological Perspective on Video Games

In this section I will focus on biological matters relating to playing video games such as physical problems caused by playing them and an interesting neurological case study of the impact of a televised version of a *Pokemon* game on viewers in Japan.

Physical Problems Caused by Video Game Playing

Let us suppose video game players spend sixty minutes a day playing a typical video game. During that period, they are exposed to an electronic medium that forces them to concentrate intensely and to expend mental and physical energy rapidly.

This concentration and expenditure of energy has certain physiological consequences. For one thing, many players become highly excited and subject to considerable stress by the events going on in the video game. In addition, long periods of play often leads to physical problems as wrists and fingers are used repetitively, so that many serious video game players suffer from physical ailments to their wrists and arms such as the repetitive stress syndrome. People who play video games two hours a day are in danger of developing chronic physical problems with their fingers (blisters), hands, wrists, and shoulders that may lead, in later years, to other serious physical problems.

A Metaphysical Aside: Who is Playing Whom?

Espen J. Aarseth raises an interesting point about the relationship between video games and players. He writes, in *Cybertext: Perspectives on Ergodic Literature* (1997:162),

> just as the game becomes a text for the user at the time of playing, so it can be argued, does the user become a text for the game, since they exchange and react to each other's messages according to a set of codes. The game plays the user just as the user plays the game, and there is no message apart from the play.

The question Aarseth raises is who is controlling whom? Is there some kind of a loss of autonomy on the part of the player, in a sense, who finds himself or herself "played with" by the game. This passage also has implications for the matter of where authorship ends and readership begins. The old division between author and reader breaks down, because the reader—or, in this case, player—plays an important role in the way the game progresses. But how much control does the player have over things? Can players do anything in games that the designers of the games didn't anticipate? It seems unlikely, though in theory it might be possible to design games that give players the power to do things not anticipated by the game designers. They would have to build a certain degree of randomness into their games.

A Possible Physical Basis for Hyperactivity?

It is reasonable to wonder whether the level excitement that some video games generate may help set the stage for hyperactivity in real life, as players unconsciously transfer their need for instantaneous satisfaction of desires and need for quick responses to commands to their everyday lives. That is, the excitement generated by the game play may lead to a need for continual excitement in real life and contribute to various kinds of behavior problems, including hyperactivity and attention deficit disorders, of one sort or another. It may be that heightened levels of physical and psychological stimulation caused by video games do not turn off suddenly but also find expression in everyday behavior.

These suggestions I've made about video games possibly leading to physical problems and to hyperactive behavior are based on statistics; my notion that these games might also lead to hyperactive behavior are hypothetical and tentative, not based on research that I know about. I'm not arguing that video games always cause such behavior in everyone but that they may contribute to such behaviors in some people in selected instances.

Who Plays Video Games

A study of video game and computer game players commissioned by Computec Media (752 U.S. and Canadian men and women between sixteen and forty-four years of age) discovered that of the people surveyed:

> 80 percent of North American gamers are between sixteen and thirty-four
> 46 percent of male gamers have a college education

31 percent of male games earn more than $50,000 a year
the average adult gamer is twenty-six years old

The survey distinguished between what it called "game players," who have fun playing games, and "game centrics" who play games as a serious hobby. The small number of respondents suggests there is quite likely a large margin of error. In addition, the survey only was given to gamers between the ages of sixteen and thirty-four, so it cannot claim to be representative of gamers in general. It neglects children who play video games. An article on this survey by David Lazarus (*San Francisco Chronicle*) concludes, interestingly enough:

> There isn't any mistaking computer games as a group activity. No matter what their other interests, the majority of gamers said they play such games alone.

Though gamers may not fit the stereotype of the sociopathic loner, Lazarus points out, they do spend lots of time by themselves, when they are playing video games.

Other researchers, such as Robert Kraut at Carnegie-Mellon University, have done research that suggests that people who spend a great of time online (and by extension we can add playing video games) don't talk to people, including family members, as much as they used to, before getting involved with the Internet, and also indicate that they feel more stressed out and depressed. A recent study of people who spent a lot of time on the Internet yielded similar findings—they tend to become depressed and alienated and spend much less time than those not so involved in the Internet with their families and friends.

Flashing Lights and Neurological Problems in Japan

There is also the matter of exposure to rapidly flashing lights and powerful sound effects that may have important neurological and physical effects, similar to those suffered by people who have attended many rock concerts and listened to music that was too loud—they suffer serious problems with their hearing. Powerful lighting also can cause problems such as headaches, minor seizures, and temporary blindness. A television program in Japan in 1977 showed a scene with a flashing light that had enormous impact; a large number of children who were watching the program started having bad headaches and various other neurological problems

On December 17, 1977 children and adults who were watching a popular Japanese cartoon show, *Pokemon,* on television were exposed to a scene in which a bomb exploded. This was depicted by having brilliant red and blue lights flash on the screen, alternatively, for approximately five seconds. Shortly after this, a large number of people who were watching the show experienced things like dizziness, vomiting of blood, seizures, migraine headaches, shaking, convulsions, and loss of consciousness.

More than 700 people were taken to hospitals in Japan in what has been described as an outstanding example of photo stimulation leading to medical problems on a mass scale. Some victims had serious breathing difficulties and had to be put into intensive care units. A number of medical specialists in Japan described the event as "optically stimulated epilepsy," which suggests how powerful the impact of the flashing lights scene was.

The scene involved using two commonly used cartoon techniques; first, it used alternatively flashing, different-colored lights (in this case, red and blue) and second, it flashed a very strong beam of light onto the screen. A doctor in Japan who treated some of the victims said the symptoms of a number of the patients reminded him of those some children experience after playing certain video games. So there may be rather powerful effects, neurologically speaking, from playing certain video games—effects that the makers of the video games are unaware of and cannot anticipate.

I should add that there are some media researchers who claim the outbreak was due to a mass hysteria and that the flashing lights didn't cause the physical symptoms mentioned above. It was, they argue, hysteria and contagion, not flashing lights, that led to the outbreak of illness in Japan.

A neurologist I know has suggested that video games may affect changes in neural pathways in players, in a manner somewhat like biofeedback. It is the physical aspects of the games—their lights and sounds rather than the narrative elements of these games—that are important here. It is possible that these games imprint certain pathways to the brain that have an effect on the behavior of players. For example, certain colors may become associated with certain kinds of behavior, and this "conditioning" is separate from what players learn from the narrative content of the games they play. This "conditioning" must be seen, of course, as an unintended consequence of the design of the game.

Game Playing and Obesity

Another biological impact of playing video games is that they may help contribute to obesity. A report released by the American Academy of Pediatrics in 1990 pointed out that by the time a person reaches seventy, he or she will have spent around seven years watching television. To this we must add the time playing video games. Research indicates there is a strong link between heavy television viewing and obesity and I would suggest that video game playing exacerbates the problem. Children aren't getting enough exercise, aren't interacting with friends enough, and are eating too many fatty snacks.

A Psychological Perspective on Video Games

In this section I deal with one of the most common criticism of video games—that they are full of violence and lead to violent behavior in those who play them, especially children.

The Problem of Violence

One of the most common topics dealt with in discussing video games and the human psyche is the matter of violence. Most video games are violent, and some, such as wrestling games, have nonstop violence most of the time. So the question arises—does playing video games lead to violent behavior in players? A 1990 report by the American Academy of Pediatrics suggests that "a steady diet of violence" on television causes some children to believe that "if you're the good guy, violence can be acceptable" as a means of solving problems. In children's weekend shows, there are an average of twenty-five violent acts per hour. Video games, I believe, only help exacerbate the problem of violence in the media.

Mortal Kombat

Mortal Kombat, when it first appeared, attracted a great deal of attention. It sold around 4 million copies between September 1999 and the end of 1999. One of the characters in the game, Johnny Cage, uses a powerful uppercut blow to decapitate his victims. Another character, Kano, rips out the hearts of his victims. And the lone female character, Sonya Blade, a victim who is at the tournament against her will, kills with a "burning kiss of death." An Asian mystic, Rayden, electrocutes his victims and Sub-Zero tears the heads off of his victims and displays them, for all to see, with the spinal cord still attached to the bloody necks of his victims.

These characters are all involved in a martial arts tournament, which sets the stage for their violent behavior. The question that arises is— should children play games full of cruelty and sadism? Although this is a video game and therefore seen by its players as not "real," there is reason to suspect that young people who play this game may become desensitized and more open to being aggressive and violent in their everyday lives.

Violence, of course, is a very complicated phenomenon. For example, there is a difference between real violence (you see someone actually shoot someone else) and mediated violence (you see a show in which a character pretends to shoot someone else). When we watch a television program, or play a video game, the violence has a different status for us than real-life violence does. Most people never see anyone killed in real life, but see thousands of killings in films and on television, and "kill" dozens and maybe even hundreds and thousands of people, monsters, and aliens, when playing video games. Thus, the fact that violence is mediated and not real gives it a different status— that of "play" or "fake." But is "play" violence less significant, in terms of its effects on us, than real violence? This is the subject of considerable debate by researchers.

Other Aspects of Mediated Violence

Consider, for example, professional wrestling on television. Most people recognize that it is a kind of theater, but that doesn't prevent them from getting excited about what happens in a match. The same could be said for other television programs that are full of violence and films, as well. So just because something is not real doesn't mean it doesn't have the capacity to excite us . . . and maybe affect us in ways we aren't aware of. Think of the power of movies and plays to provide us with powerful emotional experiences. We know that films and plays are "fake" but these works still often profoundly affect us.

Then there is the difference between "comic" violence, which we find in many animated cartoons and video games, and "serious" violence, which we find in cop shows and some video games. Does the fact that the violence is comic mean it has less impact upon our psyches? There is some question about that, and people who think that comic violence, because it is comic, is of no consequence are, I would suggest, making a big mistake. Violence of any kind, I believe, has profound implications as far as our psyches are concerned and the fact that violence is comic and we tend to dismiss it makes this comic violence even more pernicious.

There is a considerable difference between televised violence, film violence, and video game violence. In televised and film violence, one watches others—those in the television program or film—behave violently. In video games, one is a participant in the action and uses violence to achieve various goals. Let's consider television violence, which is more important for our concerns because people watch television almost four hours a day. There is good reason to believe that exposure to televised violence does tend to lead to increased violence in those who are exposed to it, especially children. Is it not reasonable to assume that being a participant in a text and actually using violence or "being violent" (even if only in a fiction) has a more profound impact upon a person—especially an impressionable child or young person.

Some scholars argue that violence in films, television shows, and video games leads to a *catharsis,* a cleansing and purging of emotions so that exposure to violence according to this argument, ironically, leads to less violence. This view is countered by scholars who argue that people, especially children, tend to imitate others. They model their behavior on characters they identify with in texts they see, who often use violence to "solve" problems. There is also a great deal of gratuitous violence in video games.

One other factor involved with this violence involves the matter of children becoming desensitized to the terrible effects of violence, because it becomes so much a part of their lives. The fact that characters can be killed and then brought to life in video games gives killing and being killed a different dimension to it.

Killing someone in a video game, or being killed in one, is often followed by his or her returning to life when the game is restarted. Very young children might possibly assume this happens in real life, and thus downplay the importance of violence they may perpetrate. (Very young children, we know, can't tell the difference between television programs and television commercials.)

In addition, some players become addicted to these games—and, more significantly, to the high levels of excitement they get from playing these games. It is conceivable that the electronic excitement players get used to can lead, in some cases, to actual drug addiction, as players, constantly seeking new "highs," migrate from addiction to video games to addiction to drugs.

The addictive quality of some video games and the immersion of players in an exciting and vicariously satisfying fantasy world might also lead to certain personality problems, such as shyness, a lack of sociability, an overly developed inwardness, a strong sense of alienation from others, and things like that. Addicted video players get their gratifications from the unreal world of video games and not from the real world. They may not get enough practice in being with others and accommodating themselves to the demands of others and of society. These video games may "train" players to behave in certain ways and it is quite possible that players transfer the kind of behavior they have learned and practiced in video games to their everyday lives.

Video Games and Addiction

A communications scholar, Robert W. Kubey, offers some interesting ideas about the reasons video games are so engaging, if not addictive. As he writes in his article, "Television Dependence, Diagnosis, and Prevention: With Commentary on Video Games, Pornography, and Media Education" (MacBeth [ed.], 1996):

> As with television, the games offer the player a kind of escape, and as with television, players learn quickly that they momentarily feel better when playing computer games; hence, a kind of psychological reinforcement develops.
> But video and computer games also have particular characteristics that make children and adults especially likely to report that they are "addicted" to them. There is the general challenge posed by the game and the wish to overcome it and succeed, and there is the critical characteristic that the games are designed to minutely increase in challenge and difficulty along with the increasing ability of the player. (242)

What Kubey is arguing is that video games, by their very nature, are designed to generate increasing levels of difficulty and of satisfaction in players, which makes the games so attractive and addictive.

He continues with his discussion of the games and adds something very interesting, utilizing the ideas of a famous psychologist, M. Csikszentmihaly, about flow experiences. Kubey writes,

> Many of us are never quite as exhilarated as when we have harnessed our abilities and set them against a difficult but surmountable challenge (Csikszentmihaly, 1990). Video and computer games can offer children and adults such a challenge.
>
> Indeed . . . computer and video games offer all the essential features that we know are likely to result in a "flow" experience of intense and enjoyable involvement and a high level of concentration: closely matched skills and challenges in an activity and rapid feedback regarding one's performance. (1996: 242, 3)

Given these characteristics, it is no wonder that video games are so addictive; one couldn't design a better device for generating these "flow" experiences. Kubey tells us that video games are engaging; he isn't certain that they are addictive and writes that they are "perhaps addictive." One other factor connected to this matter of the power video games have over some players involves what might be described as some kind of "escalation effect."

Let me offer an analogy with drug taking. Drug addicts find that they have to keep increasing the amount of drugs they take to get the effects they desire; as their bodies become accustomed to the drugs, the addicts have to keep increasing their doses to get their highs. There may be something similar happening with video games. As players become accustomed to the pleasures they get from these games, they have to increase the amount of playing to obtain the same level of gratifications to which they have become accustomed.

Kubey tells readers how he deals with video game playing by his children. He sets firm limits on how much they can play and uses a kitchen timer to keep track of playing time. He doesn't put it on the computer but leaves it in the kitchen, so his children and their friends don't make too much of it. Using a timer is, in a sense, a kind of conditioning. When the timer goes off, play stops! The timer has a kind of authority that players learn to respect.

Positive Uses of Video Games

There are, of course, positive uses to which the engaging or perhaps "addictive" aspects of video games can be put. For example, the Lucas Learning game *Exploring the Gungan Frontier*, is a game, but it also teaches players about how to take care of ecosystems. In a review of the game by Jim Schneider in *T.H.E.Journal*, he explains,

> This new hybrid CD-ROM asks players to help Boss Nass (from the new film, *The Phantom Menace*) and the amphibious Gungan people of the planet Naboo set up a

new colony on a nearby moon. By releasing numerous plants and animals into different habitats, users must create a thriving ecosystem that is able to maintain itself while supplying the new Gungan city with food and supplies. . . . Overall we found the game very engaging, if not addictive. The game's graphics and animations are great, as is its music. . . . Fun and entertaining, The Gungan Frontier teaches students about the interdependence of organisms and environment, population, and ecosystem dynamics, regulations and behavior of organisms, food webs, life cycles and symbiosis. Best of all, they learn about these elements not by seeing or hearing, but by doing. (1999: 66)

Schneider's point here is that video games have the potential to give students new ways of learning by making them active participants in an ecological experiment. The game play in video games can be a wonderful vehicle for teaching children about many different things; video games are always teaching players something about life. There is nothing to say that they can't be used in constructive ways.

One problem, however, is that children tend to avoid "learning" games when offered a choice of games to play. They are more interested in being entertained than edified, but there is nothing to say that video games can't hide their teaching in an adventure game or some other game that doesn't advertise itself as a learning game.

Social Considerations Relating to Video Games

One factor that relates to the social (and psychological as well) aspects of video games involves the matter of sexuality. There are some who believe that television and other media should be censored, to prevent young children from being exposed to sexually explicit material; others disagree, saying the First Amendment guarantees freedom of speech and maintaining this freedom is more important than shielding children (if that were possible, that is) from sexually explicit material and other material that may have negative consequences. There is also the question of the amount of media to which children are exposed to be considered. It is reasonable to suggest that video games may also have positive uses; there is nothing in the art form that prevents it from being used to teach children and to promulgate positive values.

Video Games and Sexuality

In addition to violence, there is the matter of the sexual content of video games and the use of profanity by characters in video games and advertisements for these games. These problems have led the video game industry to attempt to police itself and offer ratings so parents will know something about the content of video games they purchase for their children. The industry is attempting to persuade video game retailers to restrict access to certain video games to mature players, for example.

It is estimated that teens in the United States see around 14,000 sexual references and sexual innuendoes per year on television. Once again, video games may contribute to problems caused by all this sexuality on television. (It's interesting to note that only 150 or so references to sexuality on television involve such matters as abstinence, birth control or responsibility for one's actions.) In many video games, women are seen as objects to be controlled and to be possessed—that is "commodities" to be purchased or won. These women are then available for the pleasure of the player.

Eugene F. Provenzo, Jr. discusses a famous (or is it infamous?) sexually explicit video game in his essay "Video Games and the Emergence of Interactive Media." (1997: 104,105). He writes,

> CD-ROM games such as *Virtual Valerie,* for example, allow you to enter a voluptuous young woman's apartment. Once inside you can look through her things, including her purse, her books, and even her personal copy of the game *Virtual Valerie.* The point of the game is to eventually interact with Valerie herself. In one scene Valerie appears on the computer screen wearing a see-through brassiere, panties, and hose while lying on a couch. With her legs spread apart, she asks the player to remove her brassiere, which she finds "a little snug." The object of the program is to eventually remove all of Valerie's clothes and get her into bed with you. If you don't answer certain questions correctly, Valerie won't take her clothes off. Give her the right answers and she's yours.

Virtual Valerie, of course, is not a typical video game, but it does take our fascination with sexuality close to the level of pornography. One of the most famous video game series, *Tomb Raiders,* features an animated character, Lara Croft, who has large pointy breasts, a tiny wasp waist, and long, shapely legs. (This series of four video games, incidentally, has sold something like 17 million games worldwide.) Is there something of psychological significance involved in the fact that young boys and adolescents, as well as older males can "control" this voluptuous (by animation standards, that is) woman, and determine where she goes, when she shoots guns and uses other weapons, and how she interacts with others? Lara Croft is not the only voluptuous animated female character in video games; there are many others like her, but none have achieved as much popularity.

When I was researching video games, the owner of one store said she is very popular in Japan, where, I take it, Japanese males find having a relationship with an exotic Caucasian female, Lara Croft, very exciting. It is reasonable to assume that there are all kinds of sexual fantasies generated in males when they play video games and "control" Lara Croft and other beautiful and voluptuous women. Like a number of other video games, Lara Croft will move from the world of video games to the film world; there was a great deal of animated discussion about who should be cast as Lara Croft. The actress playing Lara Croft has to be spectacularly endowed and have other qualities as well. The actress Angelina Jolie has been selected and now the *Tomb Raider* fans are waiting for the movie to be produced. (I will discuss *Tomb Raider* in more detail in a chapter devoted to the game.)

A book dealing with images of women in video games was published in 1998 with the title *From Barbie to Mortal Kombat: Gender and Computer Games*. The editors of this book, Justine Cassell and Henry Jenkins point out that video games are dominated by men, and quote one study (Provenzo, 1991) to the effect that 92 percent of the video games had no female roles in them at all. The remaining 8 percent or roles were divided between damsels in distress (6 percent) and women with active roles in the texts (2 percent).

In their chapter "Chess for Girls? Feminism and Computer Games," Cassell and Jenkins quote a different study that sheds light on the way women are portrayed in video games. They write,

> In 1998, *Next Generation* magazine concluded that, despite dramatic increases in the number of female game characters, "they all seem to be constructed around very simple aesthetic stereotypes. In the East, it's all giggling schoolgirls and sailor uniforms, but in the West the recipe appears to be bee-sting lips, a micro-thin waist, and voluminous, pneumatic breasts."

These "Western"—that is European and American—images are the ones found in games such as *Virtual Valerie* and *Tomb Raider*. Lara Croft is probably one of the best-known exemplars of this fantastic wasp-waisted, melon-breasted stereotype.

Video Games, Media Diets, and the Problem of Ratings

The video game industry is trying to police itself because it is afraid that the federal government will create a rating system that the industry will have to follow. As a result of the shootings at Columbine High School, many parents have become alarmed about the video games their children play, as well as the music they listen to and other aspects of their media diet.

There are some questions about the media diet of young children. A recent survey suggests that children only play video games for twenty minutes a day, in contrast to spending forty-four minutes "reading for fun" (as opposed to reading for homework). But if they "only" spend twenty minutes a day, if you multiply this by seven you give 140 minutes or almost two and a half hours a week (assuming, of course, those who participated in the survey did not under-report the amount of time they spent playing video games and did not over-report the amount of time they spent reading for fun).

The incredible fact is that children eight and above spend 6.43 hours *a day* using various kinds of media—everything from listening to the radio and watching television set to listening to records and playing video games. The average child in America then puts in the equivalent of a workweek of more than forty-five hours a week involved with media. Sometimes, of course, there is multi-tasking and a child will listen to music and read a book or do homework at the same time. Nevertheless, it is quite extraordinary, I would suggest, to be involved with the media to this extent. Some of the possible consequences of this degree of involvement with the media have been spelled out above.

An early commentator on the video game phenomenon, Patricia Marks Greenfield, a professor of psychology at the University of California at Los Angeles, makes several important points in her book *Mind and Media: The Effects of Television, Video Games, and Computers* (Harvard University Press, 1984). In her chapter on video games, she suggests that the visual action involved in the games and their interactivity are two of their main attractions. As she writes,

> It is possible that, before the advent of video games, a generation brought up on film and television was in a bind: the most active medium of expression, writing, lacked the quality of visual dynamism. Television had dynamism, but could not be affected by the viewer. Video games are the first medium to combine visual dynamism with an active participatory role for the child. (1984: 101)

This is because, she reminds us, children like activities that enable them to become personally involved. She adds that other factors that children find attractive are "automatic scorekeeping, audio effects,

randomness (the operation of chance), and the importance of speed"
(1984:102). She also suggests that it is not the violence in video games
that attracts players but the action involved in playing these games,
and that violence is not a necessary component of games.

That may be the case in theory, but in practice it turns out a large
proportion of video games are violent, and in the sixteen years since
Greenfield wrote her book, they have become increasingly violent.

Video games are rated as follows:

EC   (early childhood),
E   (everyone, six and older),
T   (teens, thirteen and older),
M   (mature, ages seventeen and older),
A   (adults only).

Games also carry information about their sexual themes, violence,
language and alcohol and tobacco use. Surveys suggest, however, that
less than half of the adult population is aware of these ratings or pay
any attention to them.

Because of the violence in these games, in films, on television and
in other media, there is now a movement to adopt a more general
rating system that will cover all media; this would eliminate the confusion parents face when trying to decide whether a video game or a
film or a music disk is appropriate for their children. Now there are
different rating systems for different media and many parents find it
hard to interpret them. The corporations that create software, programs, games, and so on are caught between a desire to avoid any
governmental regulation by cutting down on the amount of violence in
their games and a desire to be free to be able to create whatever they
wish. How this issue will be resolved is hard to say.

Part 2

Analyzing Representative Games

5

Myst, Riven, and the Adventure Video Game

> *"Asked to define what they were doing, Rand used the phrase 'immersive environments.' None of them liked the word game anymore, because a game could be anything. Checkers is a game;* Riven *is an immersive environment. And the environment . . . had to be 'familiar and strange.' You had to feel that you had seen it before; you had to know that you had never seen it before."*
>
> —Jon Carroll, *"Riven." Wired.* Sept. 1997

Riven was the sequel to *Myst,* the best-selling PC video game ever made. Cyan, the company that made both of the games, sold (according to the most recent figures) around seven million copies of *Myst* and made close to 150 million dollars on the game. Cyan had trouble finding a publisher and sent it to a number of them before it was accepted by Broderbund. Game-makers need publishers to distribute and market their games in the same way that writers need publishers to distribute and market their books.

The images in *Myst* are beautiful and the experience of playing the game is very immersive. One of the reasons for this is that *Myst* has such a powerful sound design. As Janet Murray explains in *Hamlet on the Holodeck*:

Myst (1993) achieves much of its immersive power through its sophisticated sound design. Each of the different areas of the game is characterized by different ambient sounds, like the whistling of wind through the trees or the lapping of waves on

the shore, that reinforce the reality of fantasy worlds, which are really just a
succession of still images. Individual objects are also rendered more concrete by
having them ping, thumb, and whirr appropriately when manipulated. (1997: 53–
54)

Myst and later *Riven* are games that use stills that rapidly change to
give the illusion of motion. Animated films are all built on that principle, but not all of them give the illusion of reality as powerfully as
Myst and *Riven* do.

The other part of the equation, Murray points out, is that *Myst* is
"dramatically static. Nothing happens of its own accord as the player
wanders around in search of puzzles to solve" (1997:108). The lack of
dynamism in *Myst*, Murray adds, reflects the essential simplicity of
the programming in the game: "*Myst* offers the interactor an elegant
and seamless interface in which most of the activity of the game is
moving forward through a space by mouse-clicking in the direction
you want to go" (1997:108). There are few distractions when you play
the game, since you don't interact with anyone, but the price you pay
is that you aren't involved in an unfolding story.

Ironically, one of the problems the makers of *Myst* had in finding a
publisher was that they were afraid that it was too plot driven and
wouldn't sell well. Most serious gamers consider the game to have too
little in the way of plot and to be too slow-moving. We must remember, of course, that *Myst* was released in November 1993. In a rapidly
moving gaming industry, that's a long time ago.

Murray suggests that a satisfying game may not lead to a satisfying
narrative story, and offers, as an example of this, *Myst*, which she says
was "widely hailed as the most artistically successful story puzzle of
the early 1990s." She offers a brief synopsis of *Myst*:

The premise of the *Myst* story is the confinement of two brothers, Sirrus and
Achenar, in magical books that serve as a dungeon. Through a video window we
can see them in their imprisonment and hear them talking to us in short, staticky
statements. Each one warns us about the wickedness of the other and asks us to
rescue him. The brothers can only be freed by heroic labors of problem solving by
the player who must journey to four magical lands or ages and bring back a single
page from each of them for either Sirrus or Achenar. Each time the player gives
one of the brothers a magic page, he responds with a slightly clearer video seg-
ment. At the end of the game, when most of the puzzles have been solved, the
player has most likely gone to each land twice in order to gather both sets of pages
and to hear all of the messages from both brothers. At this point we are faced with
a dramatic choice. The last magic page will release one or the other of them from
the book. Which is it to be? . . . The secret of the game is that although both

brothers are evil, their father Atrus is alive and—with some more puzzle solving—can be found and rescued. (1997: 140)

Freeing Atrus, she says, is the winning ending. But there are other endings possible, which makes saying that there is a conclusion to the game somewhat enigmatic.

Jay David Bolter and Richard Grusin offer an interesting insight into *Myst* in their book *Remediation: Understanding New Media.* They argue that *Myst* is compelling and powerful because

> it simultaneously remediates several media on several levels . . . .*Myst* combines three-dimensional, static graphics with text, digital video, and sound to refashion illusionistic painting, film, and somewhat surprisingly, the book as well. Almost certainly without the conscious intent of its authors, *Myst* turns out to be an allegory about the remediation of the book in an age of digital graphics. (2000: 94)

In *Riven,* which was the wildly successful successor to *Myst,* the book also plays an important role in the game, as I will explain shortly.

In *Riven,* it is Atrus who sends the player on a mission—to rescue his wife Catherine and keep his evil father Gehn imprisoned. This is quite a family we are dealing with. Atrus's father and his two sons are all evil. It is almost as if there is a curse on the family. (I can't help but think about the curious similarity between the Greek tragedy about the house of Atreus and the name of the good figure in these stories, Atrus.)

Cyan has sold more than a million and a half copies of *Riven.* In addition to the games, there are a number of books related to the games, which have sold many hundreds of thousands of copies, as well as T-shirts and other accessories. In short, *Myst* and *Riven* have become pop culture phenomena of staggering economic proportions.

Myst and *Riven*

Jon Carroll, who has written a number of articles on the games for *Wired,* also describes *Myst,* but in a much more casual manner than Murray (*www.wired.coj/wired/archive/5.09/Riven_pr.html*). He writes,

> Gehn is the father of Atrus, who is the old guy in the cave at the end of *Myst,* also the guy who wrote all the journals in the library. Catherine . . . is the wife of Atrus. Atrus is played in *Myst* by Rand Miller.
>
> Gehn is also the son of Aitrus, whose *i* was added late in the game to avoid the confusion you may be feeling. Aitrus the elder was married to Anna, who raised

her grandson Atrus in a place called The Cleft. Meanwhile, Gehn was down in D'ni (pronounced "Duh-nee"), the great underground ruins of the ancient race who created the linking books. Gehn has learned the art of making linking books. There was a struggle between Gehn and Atrus, father and son, as told in *Myst*: The Book of Atrus, and there's all sorts of hoo-ha, including the creation of *Myst* Island by Anna and Catherine, and finally, in *Riven*, the story continues.

The person we see, when *Riven* begins, playing Atrus is Rand Miller, who with his brother Robyn, created *Myst*. Atrus is the father of two feuding sons, both of whom are evil, in *Myst*. He sends the person playing *Riven* on a mission, to rescue his wife Catherine and to keep his evil father Gehn imprisoned, so he can cause no more trouble. To help the player/hero with this task, Atrus provides a linking book. In one video in the middle of the game, Gehn explains that he is no longer an evil person and tries to "con" his way out of his prison in the land of *Riven*. To do this he needs a linking book. He is trying to make one himself but has not succeeded when the game begins.

Recently, the Miller brothers who created these games have parted ways, so we have, played out in the real lives of the creators of this mythology, a *Riven*ing—something very similar to the stories they tell in their video games. There is also an element of Oedipal conflict in the games. The basic elements of the Oedipal triangle are there: we find a son is locked in combat with his father; the son wishes to find a way to get his father out of the way and keep him away. And there is a woman involved. In this case, it is the son, his wife, and his father who are the players in this Oedipal triangle, and not the mother, but the Oedipal triangle is there and this configuration is not that unusual. Technically, in *Riven* what we have is known as the Heracles Complex, which refers to the situations in which fathers hate their children.

Heracles, or Hercules (in English), the strongest man in the world, killed his wife and children in a fit of madness. He undertook his famous labors, in which he had to do twelve seemingly impossible tasks, as a means of dealing with his sense of guilt. It might be that Hercules is a archetypal figure for the hero of adventure video games— he must accomplish many feats (which in video games means solve many puzzles) in order to triumph. In the *Myst* back-story, Gehn is alleged to have tried to kill his son Atrus.

In the evocation of sibling rivalry found in the games, there is something that has a Biblical flavor, which is understandable since both the Miller brothers are evangelical Christians. The term "*Riven*" comes from the old English and means, in essence, "to split apart." The fact that this term is used for the title suggests what the theme of the game is—a split between son and father, between good and evil.

Actually, as many reviewers have pointed out, there is relatively little in the way of plot in the game. Most of the "story" elements in the game are in the back-story and in the charge that Atrus gives to the player at the beginning of the game—in a video—rescue Catherine, keep Gehn imprisoned, and save the people on the Islands—who, with rare exception, we never see. We also gain information by reading various journals that we come across as we play the game. We learn nothing to speak of from conversation after we have been sent on our mission. After we have been given our mission, and handed a linking book, the screen goes blank and we find ourselves imprisoned in a cage.

Someone, presumably a guard, sees us and talks to us in a language we cannot understand. He seems to be confused by our inability to understand what he is saying. He reaches into the cage in which we are imprisoned and grabs the linking book we have been given by Atrus and pulls it out of the cage in which we're imprisoned. Shortly after this, the guard is hit by a poison dart and collapses to the ground. We see him being pulled away from our line of sight but do not see who has killed him. Later on we see his dead body lying in an area near the sea. This mysterious person presses a lever and the cage in which we found ourselves opens and we are free to roam around in the gorgeous but rather sterile landscape in which we find ourselves. The video ends and the game begins.

The "story" consists of our wandering around in this deserted world, in which we are—in a sense—prisoners, looking for Catherine and Gehn and having to solve various puzzles before we can achieve our goal and conclude the game. These "puzzles" are similar, in nature, to the tasks mythological heroes faced when pursuing their goals and the various difficulties heroes in fairytales face when sent on some mission.

The term "immersive experience" is very suitable for *Riven*, because it isn't a game as we commonly understand games, and there's little story to *Riven*, as well. And few other characters. The other characters are found in the videos that are found here and there in the game/story. The person who plays *Riven* is transformed into a cursor that has three powers: to see, to move, and to touch—when the cursor is transformed into a hand. In *Riven* what we do, in essence, is explore a world almost empty of human beings. It is beautiful, but in other ways it is a nightmare world, with no human contact most of the time. It is as if we are archeologists, exploring some dead civilization, except that there are some humans with whom we interact. In *Riven*, the experience is close to being autistic. We are in our own private world, so to speak, and do not communicate with others.

The quality of the drawings in the game is remarkable. We are almost hypnotized by the drawings of the landscape, the sound effects, and the haunting music. We wander about seeing things and touching them, as highly expressive music plays in the background. It is as if we are in a dream. Sigmund Freud writes, in his classic work, *The Interpretation of Dreams,*

> Now dreams think essentially in images; and with the approach of sleep it is possible to observe how, in proportion as voluntary activities become more difficult, involuntary ideas arise, all of which fall into the class of images. . . . Dreams construct a *situation* out of these images; they represent an event which is actually happening. . . . But this feature of dream-life can only be fully understood if we recognize that in dreams . . . we appear not to *think* but *experience;* that is to say, we attach complete belief to the hallucinations. (1901: 82–83)

There is a dreamlike or hallucinatory quality to playing *Myst* and *Riven*—because of the power of these images and the quality of the music.

Many reviewers have commented about the hypnotic nature of the game, about how deeply we become immersed in the world that *Riven* creates for us, about how gorgeous the scenery is and how entrancing the music is. The game seems to be a combination of mythology and science fiction, with strong fairy tale elements in it. What it lacks, some have suggested, is a satisfying plot. If it is a dream, of course, it really doesn't need much of a plot at all, since it is the experience and not the story, per se, that is important. The story actually is "revealed" in the symbols found in the dream.

A Proppian Analysis of Riven

In an earlier chapter, on the narrative aspects of video games, I discussed the work of Vladimir Propp, who did pioneering work on fairy tales. Let me list some of Propp's functions and show how they are found in *Riven*, which leads me to suggest that *Riven* has strong fairy tale elements in it—like most narratives.

Propp	Riven
Initial Situation: Members of Family Introduced	*We are told about Atrus and his family*
Villainy: villain harms member of family	*Gehn imprisons Catherine*
Lack: Member of Family Lacks Something	*Atrus lacks Catherine*
Mediation: Misfortune told, hero dispatched	*Player sent to Riven*
1st Donor Function	*Hero given magic agent (Linking book)*
Spatial Change	*Hero led to object of search*
Struggle: Hero and Villain in "combat"	*Player "fights" with Gehn*
Victory	*Player frees Catherine and imprisons Gehn*
Liquidation: lack in liquidated	*Catherine in rescued*
Solution: task is resolved	*Hero returns from Riven*

What this list shows is that many of the elements of classical fairy tales are also found in *Riven*—and, I have argued, in most narratives. What Propp did was discern the basic elements of narratives, though he was focusing only on fairy tales.

Unlike fairy tales, however, the players of *Riven* have no helpers; they are all on their own, and they encounter few people in carrying out their mission. There is a strange sense of being alone in *Riven*, of investigating a ghost civilization—there are people there, but we seldom encounter anyone. This helps contribute to the magical mood and the depth of immersion in the game. But it also makes playing it an unusually solitary experience. There is, to cite the title of Henry James' marvelous story, "The Beast in the Jungle," a "beast" in *Riven*, waiting to pounce on us as we play the game, but it hardly ever shows itself. We know that Gehn is there, somewhere . . . but we don't know when he'll attack us. So there is an element of anxiety and dread to our investigation of *Riven*.

Espen J. Aarseth has a chapter on adventure games in his book *Cybertext*. He refers to a distinction that narrative theorists make between a plot and a story:

> In the adventure game or determinate cybertext, far from moving toward a story by means of a plot with significant gaps, it is the plot that is narrowed down, by designifying the gaps. From many potential stories, a single plot is extracted (if the player is successful). (1997: 111–12)

So a video game contains many different story possibilities that players turn into plots, based on the way they play the game. The player doesn't see the story behind the plot he or she creates in playing the game.

Aarseth suggests we use the term "intrigue" to deal with the hidden elements of the plot of which the players of video games are unaware. Intrigues are elements in literary works that depend on the persons who are the subject of the intrigue being ignorant of the intrigue to be successful. In video games, the "victim" of the intrigue is the player, who must figure out what is going on. In video games, Aarseth says, players identify with the main character who becomes "a remote-controlled extension of herself" (1997:113). He adds,

> Intrigue is not locatable on any particular level of the text, or as a separate module, but it may be surmised from the overall construction and by playing. Intrigue is parallel to Seymour Chatman's concept of story: the *what* that is transmitted by the text, rather than the *way* (the *"how"*) it is transmitted. Like Chatman's story, intrigue contains what he calls events (action and happenings) and existents (characters and settings . . .) but here these ingredients are not connected in a fixed sequence. (114)

Chatman is a professor of rhetoric at the University of California at Berkeley and the author of an influential study, *Story and Discourse: Narrative Structure in Fiction and Film*.

What Aarseth is trying to do is find a way to describe the role of the video game player in creating his or her own "version" of the game while unaware of the design of the game and the constraints built into the game. There is an element of discrepant awareness involved, because players don't know how the games they play are structured and designed, and much game play involves, in essence (so many critics suggest), discovering the codes and structures in the game.

Aarseth also mentions the work of Brenda Laurel, who makes a distinction between what she calls "dramatic" and "epic" experiences. She has argued that video games provide what she describes as "first person-ness"; a first-person experience is enacted by the player, in contrast to a second—or third-person experience, which is narrated by someone else, and which she describes as an epic. In first-person games, you do things and see what happens; in second—and third-person games, you tell someone what to do and are told what happened.

In *Riven,* for example, Atrus speaks to the player in the second person; you must rescue Catherine and keep my father imprisoned, he says. This is second-person address. But as soon as the game starts and the player is transformed into a cursor, the game takes on a first-person quality, since we identify with the main character. This is made easier for us because the cursor is so abstract. We can all read ourselves into this symbol of our vision and intelligence.

Computer Games as Quasi-Films

In is article "Making Sense of Software: Computer Games and Interactive Textuality," Ted Friedman offers important insights into the nature of computer games, in general. He points out that the traditional distinction made in print fiction between the writer and the reader doesn't work with computer games, because in video games (that is, interactive games) the players actions affect the story. That is, the reader/player helps create the story. But to what degree?

Friedman explores the matter of interactivity as follows (quoted in Jones, *Cybersociety,* 1995:78):

> Although production values may have vastly improved since the days of text-based "interactive fiction," the problem that designers of contemporary "interactive cinema" face remains the same: how to define "interactive"? How can one give the player a sense of "control" over the game while still propelling the player through a compelling narrative? The solution, dating back to *Adventure* and *Zork,* has always been to set up the game as a series of puzzles. The player must muddle through the universe of the game—exploring the settings, talking to the characters, acquiring and using objects—until she or he has accomplished everything necessary to trigger the next stage of the plot. In the process, the player is expected to regularly make mistakes, die, and restart the game in a previously saved position. . . .
>
> The idea of computer "role playing" emphasizes the opportunity for the gamer to *identify* with the character on the screen—the fantasy that rather than just *watching* the protagonist one can actually *be* him or her.

Game designers can take the hypertext model and design the games so players are continually presented with a series of choices, with each choice leading to other choices. The problem, Friedman points out, is that in these games players aren't autonomous—that is, their choices "remain a limited set of predefined options . . . .the world of the game remains as predetermined as that of any film or novel" (1975:79). What this suggests is that players of video games have the *illusion* of agency, but cannot do anything that was not designed into the game. All choices players make have been predetermined by the game designer.

In *Riven,* we have a cinema-like quality that is hypnotic and immersive, but there is little interaction between the player and characters. All we do is see, touch, read, and, in the video segments, listen. For the most part, we don't find people with whom we can interact but signs of people—in buildings and artifacts. And when we do find people, in the video sections, we don't really interact with them but just listen to what they say. We are so fascinated by the world we have discovered, so charmed by the things we find, and so curious that we fail to notice that there is a sterile quality to the game. There is little interaction, and that although our emotions are stirred by the haunting music and the gorgeous images, playing *Riven* is essentially an intellectual challenge, in which we are forced to solve one puzzle after another to play the game.

What *Riven* offers us, I would conclude, is a dream world whose meaning eludes us. Like our dreams, we wonder what the characters have to do with our lives, what things mean, and how everything will be resolved. Unlike real dreams, however, *Riven* is a dream we can "remember" and return to, over and over again, by putting a CD-ROM in a player and pressing a key. If Freud was right that dreams play an important part in our emotional lives (we know that being deprived of dreams for a long period of time leads to psychological problems) then we might ask ourselves "What does this dream of sibling rivalries and Oedipal conflict, found in *Myst* and *Riven,* tell us about ourselves?"

That may be the real mystery to be solved in these games.

6

Lara Croft and the Problem of
Gender in Video Games

> *"The problem with Lara is that she was de-*
> *signed by men for men. How do I know this?*
> *Because Lara has thin thighs, long legs, a waist*
> *you could encircle with one hand, and knockers*
> *like medicine balls. Show that to a guy and al-*
> *though he may not admit it (since he suspects it*
> *may be sad to fancy a character in a game),*
> *deep down he finds Lara pretty sexy. Show that*
> *to a woman and she will complain that Lara is*
> *anatomically impossible. Which is true, because*
> *if you genetically engineered a Lara-shaped*
> *woman, she would die within around fifteen sec-*
> *onds, since there's no way her tiny abdomen*
> *could house all her vital organs.*
> *More to the point, thin women do not have*
> *big jugs. Period. Breasts, as any woman knows,*
> *are composed mostly of fatty tissue, and one of*
> *the hazards of dieting is that your tits get smaller*
> *before your bum does. Any woman who is skinny*
> *and appears to have big hooters is either a)*
> *surgically enhanced, or b) wearing a Wonderbra*
> *with padding in it. End of story."*
>
> —Cal Jones, reviews editor for *PC*
> *Gaming World* (Cassell and Jenkins
> 1998: 338–39)

Eidos International, the maker of the *Tomb Raider* video games, offers players a brief biography of Lara Croft in the booklet for *Tomb*

Raider II that one can print out from the CD-ROM. (This is sheer speculation but the name "Lara" might possibly be related to the Latin term *Lar* that means a tutelary deity or spirit from an ancient Roman household. Her last name "Croft" refers to a small farm. Her first and last names connote "naturalness" and perhaps a tie to someone with great powers who can teach us [tutelary] about life.) Lara might also be a modified form of Laraine or Laura. Her name may, of course, have no symbolic significance at all.

Lara Croft's Biography

Eidos introduces Lara Croft to us in the manual for *Tomb Raider* II as follows:

> Lara Croft, daughter of Lord Henshingly Croft, was raised to be an aristocrat from birth. After attending finishing school at the age of 21, Lara's marriage into wealth had seemed assured, but on her way home from a skiing trip her chartered plane crashing deep into the heart of the Himalayas. The only survivor, Lara learned how to depend on her wits to stay alive in hostile conditions a world away from her sheltered upbringing. 2 weeks later when she walked into the village of Tokakeriby her experiences had a profound effect on her. Unable to stand the claustrophobic suffocating atmosphere of upper-class British society, she realized that she was only truly alive when she was travelling alone. Over the 8 following years she acquired an intimate knowledge of ancient civilizations across the globe. Her family soon disowned their prodigal daughter, and she turned to writing to fund her trips. Famed for discovering several ancient sites of profound archaeological interest she made a name for herself by publishing travel books and detailed journals of her exploits.

This description offers us a number of things to think about. First, Lara is from an aristocratic British family and in her youth was sheltered from the real world by attending a finishing school.

We see elements of the Tarzan story here. He is an aristocrat whose plane crashes deep in an African jungle and he learns how to survive in it, and spends the rest of his life fighting villains of one sort or another. British aristocrats seem to have a genius for surviving plane crashes in remote areas and for living by their wits. It also helps that they are both smart and powerful (Tarzan) or beautiful (Lara Croft).

There is also an element of the Indiana Jones story, since Lara becomes a combination writer-archaeologist who discovers a number of important sites. She is, however, an amateur one, unlike Indiana Jones, who is a professor and teaches archaeology, when not engaged in his adventures. She is not, we see, an educated woman who attended a university such as Oxford or Cambridge. Aristocratic women go to finishing school where they are taught how to live the life of an idle aristocrat.

She is "disowned" by her family, for not marrying and entering into the life they thought appropriate for her—a stultifying and claustrophobic life that would presumably be spent married to someone from an equally aristocratic family. She is saved from this fate by her fortunate plane crash. Lara thus becomes independent and makes a living by writing books about her travels and journals about her exploits. Her travel books pay for her archaeological exploits.

As I mentioned earlier, many narrative theorists have argued that narratives involve travel through space, so having a job as a travel writer and being an adventurer makes it easy for her to move around the world and explore all kinds of strange lands. Many video games are narratives but they are, more importantly, explorations of strange territories. Her occupation, as a writer and adventurer, and her skills as a fighter, enable her to undertake the missions she is sent on. We always see her with two guns by her side, though she obtains the use of other weapons from time to time. The game player, of course, controls her actions.

What Lara Can Do

There are a number of actions that the player can have Lara perform:

1. Running and turning
2. Walking
3. Side Stepping to left and right
4. Rolling—she dives forward and finishes facing in the opposite direction
5. Jumping (including grabbing tricky ledges)
6. Diving
7. Swimming—underwater or on the surface
8. Shooting
9. Climbing
10. Picking Objects Up
11. Using Switches
12. Pushing and Pulling Objects
13. Looking around

We can see that Lara Croft can do any number of things—all of which are controlled by the player pressing various keys on the keyboard. In later games, she is given other skills, as well. This means players can control, determine the behavior of, have "power" over, a voluptuous woman (animated cartoon figure that she is) and can make her do all kinds of things on the screen (and who knows what in their imaginations). Technically, the *Tomb Raider* series can be described as a combination of third-person shooter and adventure game.

Some Reviews of Tomb Raider

There are countless reviews of *Tomb Raider* on the many sites devoted to video games, in general, and *Tomb Raider*, in particular. Let me offer a brief sampling of these reviews.

In a review titled "Chills, Thrills, and Frills," Jacob Ward discusses his encounter with Lara Croft in *Tomb Raider* II:

> I spent many hours in the company of Lara Croft, the treasure-hunting heroine of *Tomb Raider*, when the game was released, and now its sequel is wreaking havoc on my social life.
>
> The opening scenes depict villagers defending the Great Wall against evil Mongols and a fire-breathing dragon; when a helicopter drops Lara at the battle scene centuries later, the game takes on a foreboding sense of history and danger. On her quest for the Xian dagger, Lara travels to a variety of exotic locations—the alleys of Venice and the overturned hull of a sunken ship. In her path stands an evil cult and its insane leader, plus half of Tibet.
>
> The perspective in this game follows Lara like a camera, and the effect is nerve-racking. When she rounds a corner and brandishes her guns, you can't see what's coming until she charges into the face of danger. The effect is that of being a weak-kneed documentarian; you follow her blindly—as the soundtrack swells and your friends leave. Lara Croft has claimed, it seems, another "victim."

I might point out that other reviewers weren't as taken with *Tomb Raider II* as Ward was. The consensus of the reviewers was that *Tomb Raider II* added little to the original game, except that it provided players with another opportunity to gaze upon this voluptuous cartoon character and control her actions.

A report on the *Tomb Raider* series, found on another web site offers some insights into the role national character plays in designing video games. This report says that the American version of *Tomb Raider IV* was "dumbed down" for American kids, because they don't have the patience to solve difficult puzzles in video games. The report says that American kids have "nanosecond attention spans" so the puzzles have to be much easier for American kids than for kids in other countries.

According to British researchers, the reason this "dumbing down" is necessary is that market researchers have discovered that Americans tend to play video games for short periods of time, in between periods of watching television, so the puzzles have to be relatively simple to solve or Americans will lose patience with the game. The report also claims that Eidos, the British company that makes the *Tomb Raider* games, changed the ending of *Tomb Raider IV* for the Japanese public because Japanese players didn't want to have Lara killed at the end of the game, which happens in the British version of the game. It seems that America isn't the only "happy ending" country. Of course, killing off a hero or heroine in a video game doesn't mean that much since they are easily brought back to life.

Lara Croft, Scopophilia, and the Male Gaze

This matter of the control of a beautiful woman, with very large breasts, a wasp waist, and long legs, is something that bears consideration. There can be little doubt that there is an element of sexual pleasure that male players gain from playing *Tomb Raider* and making Lara Croft jump, turn, bend, and so on.

The term for this kind of sexual pleasure from looking is "scopophilia," which means, literally, looking (*scopo*) and loving (*philia*). It is a reversal of exhibitionism, in which one gains sexual pleasure by displaying one's body. There are two forms of scopophilia. Active scopophilia involves gaining pleasure by looking at others—in particular, their sexual organs; passive scopophilia involves gaining pleasure by being looked at by others, or in simpler terms, exhibitionism.

We don't get to see Lara Croft's sexual organs, but we do see her oversize breasts and her body, as we move her around and that is where the scopophilia comes in. One review of the game made her sexual allure quite explicit. The reviewer writes (Nov. 99, 1999 *Absolute PlayStation International Review*), "Love her or leave her, you simply can't ignore her (not with breasts that size.)" There is a rather strange symbolization involved with Lara Croft: she wears pigtails, associated with being a child, and she is voluptuous, with large breasts, signifying her being a woman. It may be that combination that players find so intoxicating: innocence and voluptuousness, the child and the sexpot.

As another reviewer put it:

> But who's kidding who? The reason most gamers came back, aside from a secret, archaeological desire to spelunk, was to lead buxom Lara through a never-ending series of catacombs and labyrinths.

It is leading buxom Lara around that seems to be one of the main attractions of the game—if not the main attraction, for many players. In some respects Lara resembles an animated version of the Barbie Doll, which also has exaggerated breasts. And Lara can be thought of as a disguised and animated Barbie Doll that males can play with and lust after—though they probably would not recognize that Lara is a disguised version of a Barbie Doll.

The Barbie Doll, in turn, is a reflexion of the increasingly anorexic image we find in popular culture of what the desirable woman should look like. It has been estimated that if Barbie were a real woman, she'd be around five foot, eight inches, have a thirty-nine-inch bust, thirty-six-inch hips and a twenty-three-inch waist.

A study of the body mass index (BMI is the weight of a woman, in pounds, divided by her height, in inches) of Miss Americas shows that they are increasingly thinner and thinner. Thus the first Miss America, Margaret Gorman, had a BMI of 20.4 while some recent Miss Americas had body mass indexes of 17.8 (Vanessa Williams in 1984) and 16.8 (Susan Akin in 1986, had the lowest BMI). From 1966 to 1991, every winner of the Miss America context at a body mass index of less than 20. Interestingly, in the 1990s, the BMI for Miss Americas has started to rise, as a more athletic image of the beautiful woman has started to become popular. Lara Croft, as an active and athletic woman, would fit into this pattern, though she is a highly exaggerated physical specimen only possible in men's fantasies.

St. Augustine, an early Church father, argued that males are unable to control their sexual passions and when seeing a woman with large breasts who revealed her body to them. He wrote:

> This lust assumed power not only over the whole body and not only from the outside, but also internally: it disturbs the whole man, when the mental emotion combines and mingles with the physical craving resulting in pleasure surpassing all physical delights. So intense is the pleasure that when it reaches its climax there is an almost total extinction of mental alertness: the intellectual sentries, as it were, are overwhelmed.

St. Augustine wrote this more than a thousand years ago but his argument, exaggerated as it is, has some logic to it. We can become, without being aware of what is happening, lustful or hyper-eroticized when we play games like *Tomb Raider* with nubile young women with large breasts.

For male adolescents and older males of color who play the game, there may also be the fantasy of the beautiful white woman who succumbs, in their erotic fantasies, to the player. We must keep in mind that we are dealing with a highly stylized animated cartoon figure, but that may not be terribly significant once a player becomes involved in the action of the game. For people of color, the fact that she is a Caucasian aristocrat may make subjecting her to their scrutiny and ultimately "conquering" Lara even more significant.

Toby Gard, who created *Tomb Raider* for Core Design, tells us what he tried to do when he created Lara (quoted in Cassell and Jenkins 1998: 30):

> Lara was designed to be a tough, self-reliant, intelligent woman. She confounds all the sexist cliches apart from the fact that she's got an unbelievable figure. Strong, independent women are the perfect fantasy girls—the untouchable is always the most desirable.

The editors of the volume point out that there is

> an underground industry in home-developed nude shots of Lara Crofts [sic], including a Nude Raider web site, and rumors that someone has developed a hack which allows one to play the game with a totally nude protagonist. (30)

They add that game magazines explain the success of *Tomb Raider* entirely in terms of Lara's erotic appeal to young males who play the game. Other theorists have suggested that there are elements of transgender identification at work in male players who play the game, who can do so without any risk of the lessening of their sense of male potency.

This matter of the way men look at women is a subject that is of considerable interest to feminist theorists, who write about what they call the "male gaze." Video games such as *Tomb Raider*, with a sexually inviting and voluptuous heroine, of course, allow an undiluted male gaze. Feminists argue that one of the basic problems with the mass media is the way women's bodies are sexually exploited—in advertisements and commercials, in television programs, in films—and to this we could add, in video games.

According to many feminists, we live in a male dominated phallo-centric society—in which the institutions of society are shaped my male power and male sexuality, and indirectly and unconsciously by the male phallus. (Consider, for example, the symbolic significance of males playing video games that they control with their "joysticks" and you can probably understand what I am talking about.)

The fact that players of *Tomb Raider* have "power" over Lara Croft and can make her do all kinds of things would be a good example, many feminists would argue, of the phallocentric nature of our societ-ies. Players, of course, do not recognize this; they are only out to have fun and are unaware of the unconscious psychological significance of what is going on when they play *Tomb Raider* or other video games. It is worth noting that the first model for Lara Croft ended up posing nude for *Playboy* magazine. There was a great deal of interest in the actress who would be cast as Lara Croft in the forthcoming *Tomb Raider* film, since she had to be—at least in the imagination of the gamers—a woman of spectacular endowments. Angelina Jolie was given the role.

This emphasis on Lara Croft's breasts suggests an element of Oedi-pal attachment in male players, who might be said to see a beautiful woman as a representation of their mothers, whose breast was the source of nourishment and connected to their earliest experiences of and feelings of love. Why should big breasts in women be tied to being seen as sexy or voluptuous if these breasts didn't, somehow, call forth memories of the breasts of the players' mothers? Breasts are, after all, connected directly in reality and in the popular imagination with motherhood and that which is maternal and not with that which is sexual—except, that is, in situations in which elements of the maternal and sexual are unified, namely in Oedipal relationships that linger in the masculine unconscious.

Lara Croft's body is typical of the current ideal of what a beautiful woman should look like. Myra MacDonald points out, in *Representing Women,* that our notions of what a beautiful woman should look like change over time:

> Notions of the ideal white female body have undergone a number of transforma-tions through time . . . In the Renaissance period, as has often been pointed out, the ideal female body, depicted in oil paintings of the time, was full and well-rounded. By the Victorian era, the maternal roundness was pinched into the hour-glass

figure, in triumphant tribute to the achievements of corsetry. During the twentieth century, change has increased in pace, with the 1920s Chanel-and Patou-inspired boyish flapper image giving way in the 1930s to the slinkier, bias-cut look, and being reversed totally in the post-war "new look," let by Christian Dior. Curvaceousness remained the norm throughout the 1950s, but rapidly gave way in the 1960s to the "Twiggy" look, as hemlines rose dramatically and the age of the mini-skirt arrived. The ideal of the slender body has remained supreme since then, although fashion continues to dress it up in novel and distinctive ways. (1995: 199)

These changes are tied to the evolution of the fashion industry, MacDonald adds, but the changes are not the result of a male conspiracy. Lara Croft has the slender, boyish body that is fashionable now.

But she also has very large breasts, which soften her image as a gun toting and therefore, in a sense, hyper-masculine adventurer, and her pony tail which makes her seem more youthful, and give her a kind of drum majorette look. Women with guns have, it could be said, appropriated or stolen the male phallus and thus are objects of dread and anxiety—they are castrating bitches who want, it seems, both their femininity and guns/phalluses, the twin sources of masculine power.

The comic book *Barbarella* was instructive in this regard. In one episode, Barbarella, one of the earliest long-legged glamorous sexpots, used her sexuality—that is, she used sex—to weaken and exhaust a soldier, after which she seized his weapons and killed him. So women are dangerous and women with guns are even more dangerous and represent threats to men, threats which males generally do not recognize except at the most superficial level.

An early Church father once said that a woman is "a temple over a sewer." This statement reflects the ambivalence many men feel about women. They are temples—beautiful and desirable. But women are also sewers— dirty and unpleasant, or in our terms, dangerous and threatening. We are attracted to women, but that attraction can be fatal.

In *The Mechanical Bride* Marshall McLuhan reproduces two advertisements showing women in undergarments—one for a girdle company and the other for Ivory Flakes—and writes:

These two ads help us to see one of the most peculiar features of our world—the interfusion of sex and technology. It is not a feature created by the ad men, but it seems rather to be born of a hungry curiosity to explore and enlarge the domain of sex by mechanical technique, on one hand, and, on the other, to *possess* machines in a sexually gratifying way.

What McLuhan wrote about possessing machines can be extended to voluptuous characters like Lara Croft, who, I would suggest, video game players attempt to "possess" in sexually gratifying ways.

7

Half-Life and the
Problem of Monsters

> *"Most developers working in 3D action will ad-
> mit that they've had to drastically rethink their
> design concepts based on* Half-Life's *radical
> redrawing of the genres landscape. Never be-
> fore has a game so significantly raised the bar
> in terms of expectations for what action gaming
> could—should—aspire to. Indeed, the term
> 'first-person shooter' almost seems too unso-
> phisticated and crass to do the game justice.*
> —*PC Gamer* Nov. 1999, p. 119.

Half-Life marked a revolutionary development in video games. Although technically speaking, it is a first-person shooter, it has enough
narrative content to it to enable one to classify it also as an adventure
game. It is best thought of, I would suggest, as a mixed-genre video
game. *PC-Life* (Nov. 1999, 119) ranked it number 1 in its list of the
fifty best PC video games ever made. In its review, it indicates that
Half-Life has strong elements of the adventure genre in it:

It would be easy to continue waxing lyrical about *Half-Life's* estimable work with
interactive storytelling and cinematic atmosphere, but all of that would be for
nothing if it weren't for the sheer bloody brilliant level and enemy design that is
the game's foundation. Massive, fiendishly constructed and beautifully rendered
environments, stunning artificial intelligence that's actually smart enough to outwit
the player time and time again; monsters that seem to always know the exact
moment to launch a coronary-inducing surprise attack; inspired multi-layered puzzles
that strike just the right chord between frustration and satisfaction . . .
  This sublime combination of rich design and powerful atmosphere make for a
unique single-player game that, like a truly great movie or book, bears being

experienced from beginning to end again and again; the many standout moments never seem to lose their impact.

PC Gamer was not alone in its praise for the game. It was awarded the game of the year prize by more than forty publications, so obviously, it struck a resonant chord.

It its Game of the Year edition, it includes a *Team Fortress Classic* program that also makes it an excellent multiplayer game (for up to thirty-two players) that *PC Gamer* described as being "virtually devoid of flaws." In short, the game has received rave reviews from many video game publications, one of which called it a "masterpiece of epic proportions" (quoted on the *Half-Life* box).

Playing the Game

There are nine different roles a player can assume; each role involves possessing different weapons and powers and has different objectives, which means the gunplay—which is what action games are all about—can become very complicated. These roles are:

1. Scout
2. Sniper
3. Soldier
4. Demoman
5. Medic
6. Heavy Weapons Guy
7. Pyro
8. Spy
9. Engineer

The game can be played at three different levels, also: easy (the monsters are weak and easy to kill); medium (the monsters are strong and easy to kill) and difficult (the monsters are strong and difficult to kill). One of *Half-Life*'s innovations is that it provides a "training room" for people who have not played action games before to build their skills.

It also uses artificial intelligence to enable one's enemies to work together and has incredible realism. As it says on the box:

Enemy Teamwork: It isn't your imagination. These guys are working together. They'll lay down cover fire, flank you and use grenades to flush you out.

Extraordinary Realism. Monsters have the most fluid and intricate motion ever seen in an action game, thanks to *Half-Life*'s skeletal animation system.

In short, Sierra Studios, which made the game, claims to have made major innovations in the action game genre and most of the video game magazines and sites seem to agree with them.

Gordon Freeman

In the owner's manual, we read a letter to Dr. Gordon Freeman (a significant name that suggests a particular philosophical point of view—that man is "free" somehow and that freedom is worth fighting for) informing him that he has been hired to work at a mysterious entity called the Black Mesa Research Facility in Black Mesa, New Mexico. He was recommended for this position by Dr. Kleiner, his former professor at the Massachusetts Institute of Technology. Let me quote a bit of the letter:

> Since you are unmarried and without dependents, you have been assigned appropriate living quarters in the Personnel Dormitories. However, you may not gain admittance to your quarters until Level 3 security processing is complete. Please bring this offer letter and all documents listed on the attached sheet to the Black Mesa Personnel Department no later than May 15. A retinal scan will not be necessary at this time, but we do require urinalysis and bloodwork to establish baselines for your medical history during your employment.
>
> Please note that as a necessary condition of your work with anomalous materials, you may be required to wear and operate an HEV hazardous environment suit. You will be trained and certified in its use during the standard orientation process.

We learn from this letter that work in the Black Mesa Research Facility is top secret—requiring a retinal scan—and dangerous. Freeman will have to wear a hazardous environment suit. We read about his background as the game starts. He received both his B.A. and Ph.D. at MIT. His freedom, it seems, is becoming more and more limited and he has to obey all kinds of rules, including wearing a hazardous environment suit and he must eventually have his retina recorded so he can be admitted to laboratories that use retinal scans as part of their security programs.

The game starts slowly. It opens on a tunnel in which a subway car is moving into the bowels of the facility. It is dark and we hear doors clanging. There is an element of danger and menace that pervades the ride, which takes something like five minutes. We can overhear a woman's voice talking about something, but it is not always perfectly clear what she's saying. At one point she indicates that the Black Mesa facility is looking for qualified people to work in certain areas. Doors continually open and clang shut.

Eventually, after wandering around a bit, the player, an avatar who takes the role of Dr. Freeman, comes upon a room in which a technician is working at a computer. He says he's going to run a test again because the results of the first run are strange. A person who looks like a scientist, with long hair, is watching him and the monitor he's working on. Further away, in the large room, another man is standing. The room is full of computer monitors, simulating our idea of what a control room in an atomic reactor might be like. This introduction to the story takes a few minutes, so the player is brought into a situation in which people at Black Mesa are confronting a problem and there is a suggestion of danger and menace, though none of the scientists seems to be alarmed at what is going on.

Images of the Scientist

In *Half-Life*, we find an interesting image of what big-time scientists are like. The Black Mesa facility is a gigantic one, with long corridors, huge doors, and many walls covered with computer screens. Some scientists work at computers and others wander around checking readouts on various computer monitors. There are enormous engines, devices emitting electrical sparks, gigantic tubes running here and there. But what is the conversation like? It is a combination of high-tech mumbo-jumbo and small talk, as various scientists say things to themselves such as "where did I put my glasses?" or ask "what happened to the donuts?"

That is, we have an opposition between the danger and high seriousness of the Black Mesa facility and the trivial everyday kind of conversation of the scientists. Players of *Half-Life* take the role of the hero of this video game, Gordon Freeman, and move him about the facility. He has to put on an HEV suit that will protect him from dangerous radiation and the player has to find the room where the suits are stored in clear cylinders, press a button on a console in the room, and move to the stage where an HEV suit will automatically be put on. Once this suit is on, Gordon Freeman can then get by a guard who prevents anyone without a suit from using an elevator. This elevator leads to the action part of the story, which eventually involves Freeman and others fighting alien monsters and also government troops, who are trying to kill him and everyone and everything else in the facility

The story of *Half-Life* has been described, in a graphic manner, by one writer. (This description, like many others I've used, is taken from the Internet.). I quote it and a review at length because it gives an excellent overview of the game. I will put the quoted material in italics, to separate it from my commentary. No author was given for the description that follows. It was found at: *www.happypuppy*.com/win/demos/halflife1/html and it was written in 1998.

Deep in the bowels of the Black Mesa Federal Research Facility, a decommissioned missile base, a top secret project is underway. A portal has been opened to another dimension, and human science has never seen anything like the world on the other side.

Here we have the fundamental issue of the story. A portal to another dimension has been opened—but nobody knows what will be coming through that portal. The question of mankind over-reaching itself, prying into aspects of life that are beyond its capacities, is introduced. This, I might add, is a common subject in science fiction stories. In some classic science fiction stories, such as *War of the Worlds,* the earth is invaded by Martian monsters and the task is to fight them and save the world. In *Half-Life,* on the other hand, it is man's meddling that has set the stage for the invasion of the monsters.

*You are Gordon Freeman, a young research associate in*the Anomalous Materials Laboratory. You have limited security clearance and no real idea of just how dangerous your job has become, until the morning you are sent alone into the Test Chamber to analyze of a strange crystalline specimen. A routine analysis, they tell you.

So far, everything is okay. The scientists wander around and Gordon Freeman makes his way to the Test Chamber to examine a specimen. The ambience is a combination, as I mentioned before, of small talk and of super-high technology, with huge computers and gigantic devices of one sort or another. The description by our Internet reviewer continues:

Until something goes wrong. Is it sabotage? An accident? Or is it something you did? All you hear is screaming; all you see is spacetime shattering. The next thing you know, the entire Black Mesa Facility is a nightmare zone, with sirens wailing and scientists fleeing in terror from the things their co-workers have become. Hordes of creatures from the far side of the portal are pouring through rifts in the local fabric of reality. Monsters are everywhere. Madness rules. You head for the surface, but the usual routes are impassable-closed off by the disaster, infested with headcrabs and houndeyes and increasingly larger and hungrier creatures.

This is the standard stuff of science fiction and one of the dominant motifs in the genre—the attack of the bug eyed monsters. The wonderful thing about aliens is that we can invent all kinds of terrifying non-human creatures and then we can destroy them without any pangs of conscience or anything like that, which explains why aliens are so prominent a part of science fiction narratives. Aliens are not creatures that humans can empathize with in any way—generally speaking—so saving the earth, and oneself as well, by destroying them, becomes a moral act.

> *As Gordon Freeman, you must enlist the help of* traumatized scientists and trigger-happy security guards to get through high-security zones, sneaking and fighting your way through ruined missile silos and Cold War cafeterias, through darkened airducts and subterranean railways. When you finally come in sight of the surface, you realize that the inhuman monsters aren't your only enemies—for the government has sent in ruthless troops and stealthy assassins. Their orders seem to be that when it comes to the Black Mesa, nothing gets out alive . . . and especially not you.

The dilemma Freeman faces is that he is under attack from both sides—from the bloodthirsty aliens and from the government, which is willing to kill him and everyone else in the laboratory in order to destroy the aliens. In such situations, science fiction heroes display both courage and ingenuity, as they find a way to survive the attacks from the aliens and the government. What we have here is an ordeal that has to be survived, which is typical of stories about heroes and heroines. The irony here is that not only are the aliens out to destroy Freeman, but so is the government—which is willing to sacrifice Freeman and his colleagues in order to contain the aliens.

> When even your own species turns against you, maybe you'll be glad to see another portal beckoning. But then again, on Earth you have allies; while on the far side of the portal, nothing at all is familiar except the sense of danger.
> Save the Earth? Well, maybe. But that's a pretty low *priority compared to saving your own skin.*

This description gives us a pretty good idea about some of the most important elements of the game. Gordon Freeman finds himself in a terrible dilemma. Everyone, it seems, is out to get him.

Another reviewer, Chris Hudak, offers a slightly different perspective on the game (from *Wired* magazine on the Internet):

> Developed by Valve, Half-Life is a first-person action/adventure game that chronicles the aftermath of an experiment gone abysmally wrong at a decommissioned missile base. As a member of the experiment team, you have made an amazing breakthrough, an alarming discovery, and a stupid decision. You are surrounded by many recently deceased colleagues and extradimensional monstrosities that you've unwittingly helped create, not to mention the all-too-human government agents looking to cover up this top-secret fiasco by killing everyone involved. To add to the fun, an entire alien ecosystem—flora, fauna, hunters, predators, the works—has taken root in the base and flourished. Your mission: make your way through to the invaders' world, thwart their plans, get back home in one piece, and find a way to reconcile with the government spooks. You won't need to find them; they'll be looking for you.

This review makes an important point, in passing. The monsters that attack are ones that we have inadvertently created, so now there is a moral dimension to the problem of the aliens—we have, by chance, created them and so must take a certain amount of responsibility for them, even though we must destroy them in order to survive. Hudak continues with his review:

> Half-Life's world is really a world—no levels or stages here, just one continuous environment through which you can backtrack. But be warned: in this dynamic environment, the places you've been may not be the same upon your return; damp walls may have grown mossy, a handful of creatures left alone may have thrived and multiplied, and ugly situations may have gotten a whole lot worse.
>
> Real-time scripted sequences add compelling plot-driven gameplay to the action; enter a chamber stealthily and you can observe patrols, experiments, discussions, and arguments in progress. Ease off the trigger finger when you encounter an alien and you may gather important clues. Or blow it away if you can, but be warned: from the craftiest military thug to the dumbest alien, the live members of Half-Life's population have the instincts to stay that way.
>
> Half-Life is a satisfying, cinematic, thinking-person's shooter. Don't just go mindlessly pumping rounds into everything you encounter—there are lessons to be learned, and the life you spare may be your own.

We can see that there is an exciting narrative element or story in this game as well as a great deal of shooting and using other kinds of weapons, but the game is not just a conventional shooter game. The important thing to notice is that shooting is integrated into a narrative. And in some cases, it is better, we discover, *not* to shoot an alien or a human being.

Half-Life as a Disaster Tale

Susan Sontag, in an influential article "The Imagination of Disaster," explains that science fiction films—and by extension we can add science fiction video games—are not really about science but about disasters. She argues that science fiction texts are very formulaic and offers some examples of the typical science fiction formula. Her first typical script involves the following phases:

1. An alien thing arrives (or collection of things).
2. The thing kills and destroys with awesome power.
3. Scientists and the military plan how to fight the thing.
4. There are more atrocities.
5. The hero scientist develops a weapon to save the world.

She offers a second basic scenario and a variation of it that has similarities to *Half-Life*:

> Another version of the second script opens with the scientist-hero in his laboratory . . . .Through his experiments, he unwittingly causes a frightful metamorphosis in some class of plants or animals which turn carnivorous and go on a rampage. (1970: 214)

In the *Half-Life* story, an experiment has made it possible for alien monsters to invade the Black Mesa facility. And the hero finds himself caught in the middle—attacked not only by the monsters but also by the government, which is intent on destroying the alien monsters and is willing, because it believes it is necessary, to sacrifice the scientists to do so.

In a sense, *Half-Life* can be seen as a cautionary tale. Scientists can make mistakes and some of the mistakes they make can place the entire world at risk. There is a good deal of dialogue in the game that has a scientific quality to it, and we see all kinds of devices doing things and monitors recording what they are doing. But beneath this façade of high technology, with talk about tests and reactors and experiments, is an important moral: scientists often make mistakes and in some cases, these mistakes place the world at risk. Therefore, we must find a way to contain scientists just as we must find a way to destroy the monsters scientists inadvertently create.

As the hero of this video game, you must do a number of things: first, you must find a way to kill the monsters—and there are many different kinds of monsters in the game, and second, you must find a way to survive the attacks by government troops. You have at your disposal a number of different kinds of weapons, of varying degrees of potency. Thus, the stage is set for a great deal of action in which your courage and resourcefulness will be put to the test.

On the Matter of Monsters

Many texts in the popular arts (and elite arts, as well) have monsters in them. The question we must ask is—why do monsters fascinate us so much? What do we "use" these monsters for, as far as our psyches are concerned. Ernest Dichter, the eminent motivation researcher, offers us some answers to these questions.

Dichter suggests that literary texts (and works of what we now would call mass-mediated culture, such as films and video games) help take care of an unconscious need people have to figure out the meaning of their lives. The mass media teach people about life and give them lessons in applied psychology. For example, people go to films, watch television programs, and play video games because they help satisfy certain needs people have—to see order imposed on the world, to have their values affirmed, to gain a sense that justice will triumph, and so on.

This leads Dichter to analyze horror films. Many of the things that Dichter writes about films apply also, of course, to video games. Dichter describes his research into horror films as follows:

> We conducted a study of horror shows and found the following: Horror films horrify and fascinate us because they show us forces out of control. What is horrifying is that the uncontrollable monster is, in many aspects, really ourselves. What is fascinating is that we would not really mind being a little bit out of control every once in a while, if only just to redress the balance.
>
> Central to all horror films today is the unmotivated lethal impulse of some kind of monster and the total inability of these monsters to control it, as well as the almost total inability of society to control the monsters. (1960: 195–96)

Dichter offers a list of some classic horror films and suggests that they all deal, ultimately, with power:

Frankenstein,	the power of the creator
The Invisible Man,	the power of omnipotence
King Kong,	the power of brutishness

| *Dr. Jekyll and Mr. Hyde,* | the power of knowledge |
| *Dracula,* | the power of resurrection |

One reason that society cannot control these monsters, Dichter suggests, is that they are really reflections of our own guilt (and society's, as well) about such things as our responsibility for having created them and for not recognizing that, in certain ways, they have elements of our humanity about them. In the same way, we are not able to admit our resemblance, in certain ways, to these monsters.

We feel a certain ambivalence about these monsters. We wonder— Is the evil found in the monster or in his creator, and, by implication, society? There are, Dichter adds, certain gratifications audiences get from watching horror films or other kinds of horror texts (on television shows, in video games, in books and so on):

> The film's society is a victim of both the monster without and the monster within. So it is with the audience watching the film. In the form of the monster, they have the vicarious and powerful expression of their own grudges against the powers that be; in the form of the monster's eventual punishment they have the vicarious and powerful expression of their own disapproval of their own impulses. (1960: 197)

So horror films and sci-fi horror video games (and by extension all kinds of mass mediated texts) have a number of meanings that are available to those who know how to interpret these texts correctly. We must recognize that our involvement with the media is connected to our participating, in a sense, in the creative process, which both gives us pleasure and helps us make sense of their lives and the world. These texts are what Dichter calls "lessons in living," though the lesson is often hidden in the text. This participation, I would suggest, reaches a very high level with interactive video games, which require players to help determine the action.

Playing the Half-Life

Half-Life is not an easy game to play; it has a relatively long learning curve. I found, for example, that it took a goodly number of hours (with the aid of various walk-through aids) for me to get Gordon's HEV suit on and find a way to the elevator. The game originally sold for around $50, which means—using the general rule that a dollar equals and hour of play, that it should take around 50 hours to finish playing *Half-Life*. I would estimate that I spent more than five hours just getting through the first part of the first segment of the story—Anomalous Materials. If *Half-Life* were a book, Anomalous Materials would be the first chapter and there would be many chapters in the book. And it would be a very long book.

8

Conclusions

Let me conclude by emphasizing a few important points that I've made in this book. Video games are, I have suggested, a major new kind of entertainment. Although they started off as very simple and primitive games like *Pong*, they quickly evolved into interactive animated works that now approach films in terms of their visual characteristics. The difference between films and video games is, of course, that films are purely spectatorial—one sees a film but does not participate in the actions, except empathetically by identifying with heroes and heroines or villains and villainesses.

Video games may mark a change in audiences, as they move from being spectators who empathize with characters in narrative texts to being game-playing participants, who now take a role in narrative texts. That is, we seem to be in the process of moving from empathy to immersion, from being spectators to being actively involved in texts. As video games become more popular, we must wonder whether our capacity to empathize with others may be, somehow, diminished. This possibility is shown in the chart below.

Film, Television Viewing	Video Game Playing
Spectatorship	Participation
Empathy	Immersion
Social cohesion	Alienation

The consequence of this development might well be the development of a sense of alienation in game players and a lack of concern for others. I will return to this subject in my discussion of bowling alone.

The Importance of Interactivity

In adventure video games one participates in the action and one's actions help shape, to varying degrees, the outcome of the game. This interactivity is built into the design of the game and is one reason for their great appeal. In some games, such as *Riven,* the visual and sound elements of the game are very important and have an almost hypnotic quality; you feel, as you play the game, as if you have somehow entered into someone else's dream. In other games, such as *Half-Life,* the dream becomes a kind of nightmare, full of monsters. There is the need for violence in this game, though the violence must be tempered by prudence, for violence can, in some cases, be counter productive.

Unfortunately, most video games aren't like that and many of them are extremely violent. As the visual qualities of the animations become better, the impact of this violence on players grows, with, I would suggest, many negative consequences—especially for young children, who play these games. They may learn, for example, that violence is the only or best way to "solve" problems and playing these games may be, in subtle ways, conditioning players to use violence in real life situations.

"Bowling Alone"—Video Games and Alienation

There is also what might be called the "bowling alone" aspect to video game playing that must be considered. "Bowling alone" refers to a problem, alluded to in a widely noted article and more recently a book, about the alleged lack of community spirit and the growing sense of isolation and alienation in America nowadays. According to the author of this article, Americans used to go bowling in groups and this signified a communitarian spirit. People belonged to many organizations and participated in numerous community activities. This spirit, the author argues, has waned and now Americans bowl alone and entertain themselves alone, or with "virtual" friends.

Video game playing is, to a great degree, a lonely activity. There are some games that are played by small groups of people and there are also games played with huge numbers of people on the Internet, but even in such cases, the people are usually separated from one another and playing in their own rooms and are by themselves. (I will shortly discuss the games that are played online by huge numbers of people.)

If you spend a great deal of time playing video games, and if, as many scholars have suggested, these games are quite addictive, it means you are not interacting with members of your family or with friends. There is, then, generally speaking, a distancing between video game players and others. Playing alone is thus similar in nature, I would suggest, to bowling alone. Playing alone may be worse than bowling alone, because when you go bowling, at least you are in a room with other people—even if you don't interact with them.

Playing video games tends to be a solitary activity that may lead to alienation and various problems caused by this alienation. The term alienation means "no connections," (*a* means no, *liens* means connections or ties) and this alienation can often lead to a sense of estrangement from others and from oneself. It's interesting to note that psychiatrists used to be called alienists many years ago.

I've suggested in my chapter on the biological, sociological, and psychological impact of playing video games, that players not only are psychologically isolated from others, but also they are likely to suffer from a variety of physical problems caused by playing these games. Players may suffer from certain ailments tied to repetitive actions by their thumbs, fingers, wrists and arms and possibly become obese, since one has little opportunity to be physically active when playing these games and a great deal of opportunity to eat fatty snacks.

The Future

As animation develops and video games approach films in the quality of their images, it seems likely that video games will evolve into a new kind of adventure film in which game players become the lead actors and actresses. How this will impact on the film industry is difficult to predict. What is also difficult to know is how being immersed into such a real-life simulation will affect players. Will video games become similar, in nature, to our dreams—that seem so realistic when we are having them? One difference between our dreams and video games is that our dreams generally help us work out problems we have, while many video games may contribute to our problems.

At the 2000 SIGGRAPH (Special Interest Group-Graphics) show, which is attended by people working in computer graphics, animation, interactive technologies and related areas, incredible advances were reported in the ability of artists to create more realistic, three-dimensional animations. An article on the show by Rick Lyman (*New York Times*, August 1, 2000, B1) noted that new developments in three-dimensional animation and very realistic special effects were leading to more powerfully immersive entertainments, both in films and video games. It is now much easier, for example, to scan photographs and other images into computers to create very realistic works of animation. In addition, the development of haptic technologies now allow video game makers to make some objects on a screen seem more real by putting vibrations or tensions onto a mouse or joystick.

Lyman quotes Roger D. Chandler, from Intel's Internet Media Initiative:

> The biggest difference we will see in the coming months is the realism. For a long time we weren't getting that realism because the processing power wasn't there on people's desktops. But now the hardware is there. And the software is becoming available to utilize it.

Ten years ago, for example, it cost around $100,000 to equip a work station to do animation. Now you can buy a computer with ten times as much power as the earlier ones for around $7,000. Many companies at SIGGRAPH were selling software to help with more realistic facial animation and animation packages at incredibly low prices that create remarkable special effects. And, of course, the remarkably powerful video game consoles that are coming on the market help make video games much more realistic and similar, in nature, to films.

Will new developments in animation lead, ultimately, to the transmission of sensual experiences—such as smell and touch—so that video games become capable of giving players sensations that people have when, for example, they are having sex? Or eating a meal at a three-star French restaurant? Or traveling in a strange land?

Will these new video games become a kind of opiate for people who can find an outlet for their sexual and other needs in simulations that seem, in many cases, better than those offered by their real-life experiences? That is the big question these games pose for the future. The French social scientist Jean Baudrillard has argued that the new postmodern societies are societies of simulation. But he didn't anticipate the remarkable technological developments in computer graphics that suggest that his critiques of contemporary culture might be, if anything, greatly understated.

It may seem fantastic to think about video games developing in such ways, but it probably seemed fantastic, when *Pong* was invented, to imagine that video games would ever evolve into realistic games like *Riven* or *Half-Life* or any of the other new games that are played on increasingly powerful game players or computers.

An Interview with Lauren Fielding

I asked Lauren Fielding, an editor at an Internet video game site, about the future of video games and got some interesting answers. First, I asked whether video games are a new art form or a new medium:

> That's an interesting question, because by separating the two, you're implying that a medium can't also be an art form. Or an art form can't also be a medium. I think these lines are blurring more and more, given the jolt of technology we've all received over the last five years. Many video and PC game artists are earning street credentials as designers in other areas, such as film, comic books, etc. And the legendary Shigeru Miyamoto (*Donkey Kong, Mario, Zelda*) is noted as the most amazing, creative mind in the industry. But I think the video and PC games industry is revolutionizing more than just art or a medium. It's revolutionizing how we look at entertainment. With the games industry grossing more than Hollywood last year, we have to wonder if people are tired of being passive spectators to various forms of entertainment. And for those who've disliked games in the past, perhaps due to their playful, unrealistic quality, well, that's changing, too. Games are quickly becoming interactive movies.

If video games are becoming interactive movies, it means that the people who play them, the gamers, will become the heroes and heroines or villains and villainesses of these new games/movies. We may find this playing so intriguing and addictive that we neglect other aspects of our lives—including our loved ones.

Then I asked about the most important new developments taking place in the design of games. Fielding's answer was quite interesting:

> Many would have you believe that the most important developments are occurring in graphics and such. But that's not really the case. I think that the new console systems and better online access are causing us to rethink games. It's not only enough to take the types of games we're used to and then enhance them graphically and so forth, developers are beginning to think about richer gameplay environments, new gaming concepts, such as music and rhythm games, persistent RPGs [Role Playing Games] and other online massively multiplayer games.

These massive multiplayer games are those that are played on the Internet by tens of thousands of people, who pay for the software to play the game and also pay a certain amount of money each month to play the game. Obviously, for game designers, having large numbers of people paying each month to play a game is better than just selling a CD-ROM of a game and not making any more money from the game.

One of the most popular multiplayer video games on the Internet is *Everquest*. It is estimated that on any given night, something like 50,000 people can be found playing this fantasy game (similar in nature to the old *Dungeons and Dragons* game children played years ago), often for many hours at a time. Players take on the roles of wizards, elves, and warriors who slay dragons and travel around the land in groups of six, get married, go on quests, and so on. They band together to protect themselves and to fight against goblins, dragons and other monsters. So there is violence in the game, though there is little violence between players.

To play *Everquest*, you must purchase a $40 CD-ROM with the game's software and also pay $9.89 a month. Players create characters and then enter the game. As they play, their characters become more and more powerful. When they reach level 39, for example, they are "clerics" who can raise people from the dead. There are approximately 200,000 people who are active players and about one quarter of them play at any given night. This game is quite addictive and many players find themselves spending hours each evening in the game. The amount of money to be made from a game with 200,000 people each paying $40 for the software and almost $10 a month to play the game is, obviously, considerable. The makers of Evequest are getting $24 million dollars a year in monthly dues and collected $8 millions dollars for the *Everquest* software.

A useful, though perhaps somewhat stretched, analogy to these multiplayer games would be in the academic or scholarly book industry. Publishers may make money on selling individual books (especially if they are used as textbooks in college courses). But it is much better for publishers to sell subscriptions to scholarly journals, because each subscription is really the equivalent of selling four books (for quarterly journals) and the publisher knows how many journals to print, so there isn't the problem of remaindered books or of carrying them on inventory.

Ironically, video games may be leading people back into some kind of a community, but it is a *virtual* community and the gratifications involved in being a member of this community aren't the same, I would suggest, as being involved in a real community. I have suggested, earlier, that new developments in animation and related matters may enable us to "enjoy" a meal at a three-star French restaurant. But after we've enjoyed this simulated meal, we still don't have a full stomach and may find ourselves hungry. I would use the same analogy for virtual communities—it isn't the same as being in a real community; our efforts aren't other-directed the way they often are in real communities and the gratifications we receive aren't the same.

It is impossible to guess where video games will lead us. They have the power to amuse and entertain us, and, better than any other medium, to involve us (when we play these games) in their narratives. But we cannot know whether, in some curious way, these games will also have serious negative consequences for us, as individuals, and for the societies in which we live. The degree to which we become immersed in their created realities may be dangerous. It is possible that they can become or will become instruments of psychic liberation and regeneration, but we may have created the instruments of our own enslavement—psychological and otherwise.

Bibliography

Aarseth, Espen J. (1997). *Cybertext: Perspectives on Ergodic Literature.* Baltimore, MD: Johns Hopkins University Press.

Barthes, Roland. (1975). *The Pleasure of the Text* (trans. Richard Miller). New York: Hill & Wang.

Barthes, Roland. (1984) *The Semiotic Challenge* (trans. Richard Howard). New York: Hill & Wang.

Berger, Arthur Asa. (1997). *Narratives in Popular Culture, Media and Everyday Life.* Thousand Oaks, CA: Sage Publications.

Berger, Arthur Asa. (1998). *Media Analysis Techniques (Second Edition)* Thousand Oaks, CA: Sage Publications.

Bolter, Jay David and Richard Grusin. (2000) *Remediation: Understanding New Media.* Cambridge, MA: MIT Press.

Card, Orson Scott. "Gameplay: Films can Make Lousy Games." *Compete,* 1991: 54.

Chonin, Neva. "Playing Virtual God: The Sims lets control freaks run characters' everyday lives," Feb, 5, 2000. *San Francisco Chronicle.*

Cotton, Bob and Richard Oliver. (1997). *Understanding Hypermedia 2.000.* London: Phaidon Press.

Coover, Robert. "The End of Books." June, 1992. *New York Times.*

Crawford, Chris. (1982). *The Art of Computer Game Design.*

DeCerteau, Michel. (1984). The *Practice of Everyday Life* (trans. Steven Rendall). Berkeley: University of California Press.

Dichter, Ernest. (1960). *The Strategy of Desire.* London: T.V. Boardman.

Herz, J.C. (1997). *Joystick Nation: How Videogames Ate Our Quarters, Won Our Hearts, and Rewired Our Minds.* Boston: Little, Brown.

Huizinga, J. (1955). *The Waning of the Middle Ages.* New York: Doubleday Anchor Books.

Jones, Steven G. (1995). *Cybersociety: Computer-Mediated Communication and Community.* Thousand Oaks, CA: Sage Publications.

Lancey, David E. and Bernard L. Hayes, "Interactive Fiction and the Reluctant Reader." *English Journal.* Nov. 1988.

Landow, George P. (1997). *Hypertext 2.0: The Convergence of Contemporary Critical Theory and Technology.* Baltimore: Johns Hopkins University Press.

Laurel, Brenda. (1993). *Computers as Theatre.* Reading, MA: Addison-Wesley.

Lyman, Rick. "Bracing for Animation's Big Leap." *New York Times.* Aug. 1, 2000, B1.

MacBeth, Tannis M, (1996). *Tuning in to Young Viewers: Social Science Perspectives on Television.* Thousand Oaks, CA: Sage Publications

McLuhan, Marshall. (1965). *Understanding Media: The Extensions of Man.* New York: McGraw-Hill.

McLuhan, Marshall and Quentin Fiore. (1967). *The Medium is the Massage: An Inventory of Effects.* New York: Bantam Books.

Murray, Janet H. (1997). *Hamlet on the Holodeck: The Future of Narrative in Cyberspace.* Cambridge, MA: MIT Press.

Platt, Charles. "Interactive Entertainment: Who writes it? Who reads it? Who needs it?" *Wired.* September, 1995.

Sontag, Susan. (1970). *Against Interpretation.* New York: Dell.

Steinberg, Shirley R. and Joe L. Kincheloe (eds.). (1997). *Kinder-Culture: The Corporate Construction of Childhood.* Boulder, CO: Westview Press.

Stephenson, William. *The Play Theory of Mass Communication* (1988) New Brunswick, NJ: Transaction.

Turkle, Sherry. (1995) *Life on the Screen: Identity in the Age of the Internet.* New York: Simon & Schuster.

Index

Aarseth, Espen J., 16–17, 55, 56, 79–80
Absolute PlayStation International Review
  Lara Croft's breasts, 87
Addiction
  video games, 63, 64
Adventure, 81
Aitrus, 75
Akin, Susan, 88
Anna, 75, 76
Arabian Nights, 29
Art of Computer Game Design, 14
Asteroids, 27
Atrus, 75, 76, 77, 79, 81 Avatars, 17, 33

Baird, Freedom, ix
Barbarella, 91
Barthes, Roland, 33, 37
Baudrillard, Jean, 108
Bettelheim, Bruno, 13, 43
Blackman, Haden, ix
Blade, Sonya, 60
Bolter, Jay David, 5, 75
Boston, Jane, 55
Brown, Michael, 8, ix

Cage, Johnny, 60
Card, Orson Scott, 10
Carroll, Jon, 73, 75 Cassell, Justine, 67
Catherine, 75, 77, 79, 81
Centipede, 27
Certeau, Michel de, 36–37, 41
Chandler, Roger D., 108
Chatman, Seymour, 80
Chonin, Neva, 13

CNET, 8
Compute, 10
Crawford, Chris, 14, 15–16
Croft, Lara, 66–67, 67, 83–91, vii, viii
  actions she can do, 85
  as Barbie Doll figure, 88
  biography of, 84
  breasts, 83, 87, 88, 90, 91
  Caucasian aristocrat, 89
  female body image and, 88
  ideal of feminine beauty, 90
  male ambivalence towards women, 91
  male gaze, 87, 87
  Nude Raider site, 89
  Oedipal aspects, 90
  power over by players, 86
  Scopophilia, 87
  self-reliant woman, 89
  treasure hunter occupation, 86
Csikszentmihaly, M., 63
Cyan, 73
Cybersociety: Computer-Mediated Communication and Community, 36, 81
Cybertext: Perspectives on Ergodic Literature, 16–18, 56, 79, 80

Dichter, Ernest, 101–102
Donkey Kong, 27, 109
Doom, 38
Dr. Jekyll and Mr. Hyde, 102
Dracula, 102
Dungeons and Dragons, 110

Everquest, 110, 111

Exploring the Gungan Frontier, 64

Fielding, Lauren, 109, ix
Focal points in studying media
   America (society), 7
   Audience, 7
   Artist, 7
   Art work, 7
   Medium, 7, 8
Frankenstein, 101
Freeman, Dr. Gordon, 95–98
Freud, Sigmund, 78, 82
Friedman, Ted, 10, 81
From Barbie to Mortal Kombat: Gender
   and Computer Games, 67
Fuller, Mary, 11, 36

Gameboy, 19
Games
   definitions of, 14, 15
   difference from stories, 15, 16
   need for conflict in, 16
   similarities with stories, 36–38
Gard, Toby, 89
Gorman, Margaret, 88
Greenfield, Patricia Marks, 68
Grusin, Richard, 5, 75

Half-Life, 93–103
   ambivalence about monsters in
     players, 102
   as disaster genre of science fiction,
     100
   Gordon Freeman's biography, 95
   images of scientists, 96, 97
   problem of monsters, 101–102
   reviews of, 97–99
   revolutionary development in video
     games, 93, 94
   roles a player can assume, 94
   Team Fortress Classic program, 94
Hamlet on the Holodeck: The Future of
   Narrative in Cyberspace, 18, 46, 73,
   74, 75
Hayes, Bernard L., 42
Herz, J.C., 9

Homo Ludens, 11
Hudak, Chris, 99
Huizinga, J., 11

I, the Jury, 5
Incredible Hulk, 46
Interactivity
   crucial element in appeal of video
     games, 15
   element in computer game design, 14
   explanation of, 9
   in narrative texts, 9
   in video games and other media, 5
   limitations of in video games, 16, 17
   new technologies and interactivity, 11
   reading and writing now mixed
     together, 10
   significant aspect of video games, 12
   video games use of, 106
Interpretation of Dreams, 78
Invisible Man, 101 James, Henry, 79
Jenkins, Henry, 11, 36, 67 Jolie,
   Angelina, vii

Jones, Cal, 83
Jones, Indiana, 84
Jones, Steven G., 36
Joyce, James, 5
Joystick Nation: How Videogames Ate
   Our Quarters, Won Our Hearts, and
   Rewired our Minds, 9

Kano, 60
King Kong, 101
King Lear, 46
Kraut, Robert, 58
Kubey, Robert W., 62, 64

Lancy, David F., 42
Landow, George, ix
Laurel, Brenda, 34, 80, ix
Lazarus, David, 58
Los Angeles Times, vii
Lucas Arts, vii
Lucas Learning, 38
Lyman, Rick, 108

MacDonald, Myra, 90, 91
Mario, 109
McCormick, Mike, ix
McLuhan, Marshall, 31, 32, 33, 38, 39,
  91–92
Mechanical Bride, 91
Media
  cool vs. hot, 33
  electronic and print, 30
  focal points in analysis of, 7
  linearity in electronic and print media
    chart, 31
  print and electronic media compari-
    son chart, 32
  print vs. electronic narratives, 31–34
Medium is the Massage, 38, 39
Microsoft X-Box, 21–23
Miller, Rand, 75, 76
Miller, Robyn, 76
Miller, Stephen C., 38
*Mind and Media: The Effects of
  Television, Video Games and
  Computers,* 68, 69
Missile Command, 27
Miyamoto, Shigero, 109
Morphology of the Folktale, 34, 35
Mortal Kombat, 35
  violence in, 60, 61
Murray, Janet H., 18, 29, 46, 73, 74, 75,
  ix
Myst, 35, 38, 73–76
  dramatically static, 74
  Jon Carroll description, 75, 76
  Oedipal aspects, 76
  remediates media, 75
  simplicity of programming, 74
  synopsis of game, 74, 75

Narratives, 29–47
  discours, 31
  future of print narratives, 41, 42
  histoire, 31
  importance of spatial relations, 36
  interactivity in, 29–40
  plot vs. story, 79
  print and electronic interactive

compared, 32–35
  print vs. electronic, 30
  Proppian functions, 34, 35
  Propp's functions chart, 45
  similarities with games, 36–38
  Tobias' 20 master plots chart, 46
  two theories of, 44–47
  uses and gratifications, 40, 41
*Narratives in Popular Culture, Media,
  and Everyday Life,* 45
Newsweek, 5
New York Times, 4, 38, 108
Nintendo, 19–24, 30

O'Neil, Kitty, ix

Pac-Man, 10, 27, vii
PC-Life, 93
Platt, Charles, 39
Play Theory of Mass Communication, 11
Pleasure of the Text, 33
Pokemon
  mass scale medical problems and, 59
Pong, 10, 22, 27, vii
Post-infantile omnipotence, 44
Practice of Everyday Life, 37
Prince of Persia, 27
Propp, Vladimir, 34–35, 44, 45–46, 46,
  78–79, 79
Provenzo, Jr., Eugene F., 3, 6, 66, 67

Quake, 38

Rayden, 61
*Remediation: Understanding New
  Media,* 5, 75
Representing Women, 90, 91
Riven, 7, 27, 35, 38, 73–82
  as an intrigue, 80
  as immersive experience, 77, 78
  dreamlike aspects of, 78
  immersive power of, 78
  Proppian analysis of, 78, 79

Schneider, Jim, 64–65
Sega, 30, viii

Sega Dreamcast, 19–24
Seinfeld, 46
Semiotic Challenge, 37
Servo-proteins, 44
Sexuality
    Tomb Raiders, 66, 67
    video games and, 65–67
    Virtual Valerie, 66
Sierra Studios, 94
SIGGRAPH, 107
Sontag, Susan, 100
Sony, 4, 30
Sony Playstation 2, 4, 19–24
Space Invaders, 27
Spillane, Mickey, 5
St.Augustine, 88
Stephenson, William, 11
*Story and Discourse: Narrative Structure
    in Fiction and Film,* 80
Sub-Zero, 61
Sutton-Smith, Brian, 11, 12

T.H.E. Journal, 55
Tarzan, 84
Television
    violence, 63
The Oregon Trail, 35
Time, 5
Tobias, Ronald B., 46
Tomb Raider, viii, 10, 27, 35, 66, 67, 83–
    92
    male gaze and, 89
    phallocentric society, 90
    problem of gender in, 83–92
Tomb Raider II
    Lara Croft biography, 84
    reviews of, 86
Tomb Raider IV
    dumbing down for American kids, 86,
    87

Ulysses, 5
Uses and Gratifications
    theory explained, 40
    print narratives vs. electronic
    narratives, 40

Video Games
    addiction, 63, 64
    aids in developing reading skills, 42
    alienation, 106, 107
    as art forms, 5
    bio-psycho-social perspective, 55–69
    cost of playing, 23, 24
    creation of, 16–18
    defined, 12–14
    design of, 14–16
    difference from film, television
        viewing, 105
    dramatic vs. epic experiences, 80
    genres, 35
    hyperactivity and, 57
    illusion of agency in, 81, 82
    immersive aspects, 9, 10
    interactivity, 17, 18, 106
    liberation or enslavement?, 111
    massive multiplayer games, 109, 110
    new developments in, 107, 108
    obesity and, 60
    physical problems from playing, 56–
        60
    positive uses of, 64, 65
    possibilities and dangers, 42–44
    problem of gender in, 83–92
    ratings, 69
    second person storytelling form, 39
    sexuality and, 65–67
    size of industry, 24–27
    solvable maze design, 18
    tangled rhizome design, 18
    violence and, 60–63
    virtual communities and, 110, 111
    where played, 19
    who is playing whom?, 56, 57
    who plays?, 57, 58
Violence
    television and, 61, 62
    video games and, 60–63
Virtual Valerie, 66, 67

Ward, Jacob, 86
War of the Worlds, 97

*Where in the World is Carmen
    Sandiego?*, 35
Williams, Vanessa, 88
Wired, 39

Zelda, 109
Zork, 81